Praise for
THE HUNT *for my* SMILE

"This book is a fabulous collection of inspirational stories. As health practitioners, we can offer the tools and education, but for true healing to take place, a sense of community and a sense of belonging is an integral piece of the puzzle. This book brings together survivors of all kinds of facial paralysis and welcomes us into each of their worlds, to hear about their journeys, challenges, and achievements. We are honored to have been a part of this project."

-Jodi Barth, President, Foundation for Facial Recovery

 FOUNDATION FOR
FACIAL RECOVERY

"This volume provides an opportunity for ordinary people to share extraordinary journeys. It provides a space in which we can retake our narratives, and find the exceptional in everyday survival."

-Dr. Faye L. Wachs, Ph.D., Author,
Professor California Polytechnic University

"As a facial therapist, I find these stories to be important and necessary to be heard by anyone affected by facial paralysis and the healthcare providers who treat them.

It is about people discovering self-love and taking control of their health and life despite misinformation and lack of proper medical attention for some... It's about coming from a place of loss, sometimes self-loathing and anger initially, to a state of acceptance, community (some changing the way facial paralysis patients are treated in their countries), positivity, and being in control of their feelings and gaining a new state of mind and approach to life.

It offers a collection of the many experiences, both physical and emotional, one can have when dealing with this misunderstood diagnosis. It is an extremely self-empowering read and should be required for all with facial palsy..."

~es Butheau, MPT, CMP

 BUTHEAU
PHYSIOTHERAPY

The Hunt for My Smile

Stories of people who lost their smile to facial paralysis, and their journey to find it again.

Amy Sameck

Amy Sameck Publishing

To Ella.
What Else Is Possible...

Contents

Elena Oleske

Thank you
for having such
a positive impact
on me. Having
had been your student
was truly a blessing!

FOREWORD

Finding our smiles inside ourselves

By Dr. Faye Linda Wachs, author of over 20 peer-reviewed publications, several book chapters, and the co-author of the award-winning book, *Body Panic: Gender, Heath and the Selling of Fitness*. Her most recent book, *Metamorphosis: Who We Become after Facial Paralysis*, is available Fall of 2023 from Rutgers University Press. She is a professor of sociology at Cal Poly Pomona and lives in Los Angeles, California.

I was honored when Amy Sameck and Barbie Wharton invited me to introduce this collection. As a person with a facial difference (synkinesis as the result of Bell's palsy), a scholar who studies bodies, and a person with a hidden disability, the stories resonated deeply. The pain, fear, shame, alienation, frustration in accessing appropriate care, and desire to hide were all things I had experienced. In this volume, people with facial differences from a host of causes come together to share the commonalities in their experiences. The most common causes of acquired facial differences are Bell's palsy, Ramsay Hunt syndrome, acoustic neuroma removal, surgery, or trauma. Congenital facial differences are usually genetic or developmental, like Moebius syndrome, but often the cause is unknown. While different causes carry a host of unique challenges, there are some overlapping commonalities in experience.

Regardless of the cause, those with facial differences face a host of physical, emotional, social, and cultural challenges. Western culture has embedded assumptions that appearance and morality are connected. Victorian assumptions that linked virtue and beauty contained deeply embedded racism, sexism, ableism, and classism, and these assumptions still persist in our culture. A visible facial difference tends to elicit, at best, interest and pity, at worst, stigma and condemnation. Exacerbated by a market system that valorizes appearance-related investments, people with facial differences are often at a disadvantage in terms of others' perceptions, which often assume rudeness, intoxication, or mental incapacitation. Stories of bullying, exclusion, discrimination, and rejection are common.

Facial differences are poorly understood. Many of those I've spoken with over the years received inaccurate information and inappropriate treatments while their mental health was neglected. It is devastating to hear many of these challenges remain, but heartening to also read of improvements to standards of care, especially better access to physical treatments and mental healthcare. Fewer than 30 people worldwide had received selective neurolysis surgery when I tried it. I was forced to pay out of pocket, but lucky enough to live less than 10 miles from one of the people who pioneered the treatment. Through his office, I connected with occupational therapists specializing in synkinesis, mapped my ideal Botox points, and had two selective neurolysis surgeries with added enhancements to create symmetry. I joined support groups and was able to lobby my healthcare provider to cover my Botox. I had no idea how privileged I was simply to be able to access specialists. The office was so close to my home that I often rode my bike. Only after I began my research did I realize that most could not access the treatments I found so helpful or attend the support groups from which I received so much compassion.

As I researched facial differences, I was struck by the assumption of exclusion, ostracism, and what one scholar termed "social death." Despite appreciating much of the scholarship, reading about my inevitable rejection was more jarring than what I experienced in my day-to-day life. It was certainly difficult to have people "notice" my difference, question my abilities, or make assumptions. I'm sure some have unkind things to say when I am not around, and many have expressed relief at not experiencing this or being in my shoes. That's all true, but in my story of self, I am a survivor. I am someone who self-advocated despite roadblocks and challenges. I navigated a sea of misinformation to find excellent and appropriate care. I joined support groups, and now I facilitate them. I live with challenges and discomfort, and I still enjoy life. This is the story I prefer.

This is why I so appreciate what Amy and Barbie have accomplished. They've let us tell our own stories. But they have also curated a collection of stories about survival. So often, I hear from newly diagnosed people that they want to heal and will do anything to recover. This collection demonstrates that even if one doesn't heal in the traditional sense, one can still grow through the experience. One can still thrive with a facial difference. Redefining healing to include living with a facial difference rather than in spite of it is freeing. It allows us to change that "wish not to be us" into an appreciation of who we are becoming.

This collection contributes in a host of ways, including personal narratives and accessible information about causes, treatments, and methods of improving comfort and mental or physical health. Ilan Livne provides one of the best explanations I've encountered of nerve damage due to Bell's palsy and the appropriate versus inappropriate treatments. Renee Hacker offers excellent advice for dealing with healthcare providers and shares how empowering it can be. Ferial Abdoel recounts surviving a major health crisis while simultaneously dealing with a facial difference. So many of the stories provide options and opportunities.

Second, the collection highlights social-emotional psychological challenges and demonstrates a myriad of ways people found inspiration, courage, fortitude, and impetus post facial differences. How did people not just "carry on" but thrive? Michael Ammons shares how he was able to reclaim his life through leadership courses, while Loriene Ezell, Reneé Ramirez, and Angel Faulk describe turning to their faith and religious communities. Hailey Dougherty shows how she found similar spiritual support through her relationship with the natural world. Kayla Tano and Andrea DiGiovanni speak of learning to prioritize self-care, while Kristiene Harp expresses how she embraced self-love. Mary Freed tells how healing began when she rejoined her valued fitness community, and Cristina Toso reminds us of the importance of rest. Describing her healing process, Maryam El Amiri expresses how she found peace of mind and optimism that had before eluded her. Cheryl Klufio invites us on her journey of growth, and Amy reminds us that our smile isn't necessarily a physical thing. Each story highlights finding ways to fortify ourselves rather than succumb. These people share their struggles on their way to survival and their triumphs in becoming someone they genuinely like more than who they were before.

Third, the collection demonstrates that social death is not a certainty and that we can and do thrive. Anayansi Arias Iriarte shows us how to find humor in our challenges and share that laughter. Terry Fox shares that despite some social rejection, the support of his friends strengthened what became life-long relationships. Similarly, Heather Pate and Maria Sias detail the profound impact that supportive friends and family can have. Elena Oleske shares the struggle to regain her self-confidence, and Tamara Weidersum shares how she found the courage to stand up for herself against her detractors with support from friends. Roshawn Dorsey describes founding a non-profit that allows her to continue her passion for the performing arts and create inclusive spaces. Despite rejection, poor choices spurred by lowered self-esteem, and barriers to inclusion, these people found ways to rebuild a social self they enjoyed.

Finally, Amy, Barbie, and all the contributors in this collection are part of creating a proactive community, advocating for inclusion and our needs. For too long, those with facial differences have been rendered silent in the discourse. Popular culture features those with facial differences suffering exaggerated trauma (Phantom of the Opera), employs facial differences as a signal of villainy (many James Bond villains have facial differences), or highlights only those deemed "exceptional" (Wonder). This volume provides an opportunity for ordinary people to share extraordinary journeys. It also creates space to retake our narratives and find the exceptional in everyday survival.

The resiliency of people healing from facial paralysis and living with synkinesis and other side effects, my own included, is a source of endless inspiration. Bearing witness to others' growth through pain is a compelling reminder that we can be the change that makes the path easier for those who follow us. I hope that those with facial differences, those who work in healthcare, those who care about people with facial differences, and the general public become more aware of the experience. The challenges so many of these authors are brave enough to share can be mitigated. We can't undo what happened, no matter how much we may want to. But we have all grown through this experience. We've learned to advocate, expand our compassion for others and ourselves, overcome barriers in communication and social interaction, and educate. We've proven ourselves resilient, and despite significant challenges, have retained an ability to be happy. This volume rejects the idea of pity and instead invites the reader to join us on our journeys as we overcome. In sharing her story, Barbie reminds us that there is no perfect, no ideal. There's just us, living our lives the best we can. We hope that work like this will expand our community of support and understanding.

-**Faye Linda Wachs**

INTRODUCTION

Why The Hunt for My Smile?

Amy Sameck

Lithia, FL, USA

Dear Reader, I decided to address you directly to introduce the reason behind this book. It is so much more than twenty-four people sharing their experiences of facial paralysis and how they survived those early days when they were full of fear and the unknown. This book was birthed for readers who don't have the opportunity to seek medical assistance immediately upon onset (many don't even know that they should). These same readers may not have top-notch insurance that covers treatments such as ENT visits, physical therapy, and botox, much less counseling with someone experienced in facial paralysis and all that comes with it. And while social media is growing its awareness and has good intentions, it's not always a safe place to be, and the accuracy of the information you get there is uncertain.

When my paralysis started, I searched for a self-help book to offer me guidance and support and was left wanting. I didn't find a "how to" book for learning to live with facial paralysis, much less a community of people who shared their experiences in a way that I felt connected to, and I was left feeling isolated and alone. I joined a few groups online, but they mostly left me scared and confused. I felt there was nowhere to turn to for help with what I was going through.

When the idea for the book came to me, I had just written my own story for a collaborative book about surviving through difficult times and still maintaining joy. Within a few weeks of writing, I realized that I experienced healing from putting my words on paper and sharing them with the world. I thought about how there was a lack of published works for me to read when I was new to paralysis, and that sparked the idea of filling the literary gap. The written word is powerful. It can offer comfort, provide understanding, and give power to the reader. So the intention for this book was born. By creating a place for stories to be shared, information spread, and awareness seeded, we hope to be where the journey to finding *your* smile begins.

This book is not medical advice, but it is educational, and you will receive nuggets of information from real-life people living with facial paralysis. You will find suggestions for medical professionals who have experience with treatments that could help your recovery, as well as some warnings to stay away from treatments that could cause more damage to the facial nerve. This book also offers support for those who are walking this new life alone. Every author gives you a way to follow or get in touch with them and shares how they are navigating their journey with tips and tricks for living happily and well with facial paralysis. You can learn from their mistakes and triumphs – and you won't be alone.

The Hunt for My Smile isn't just about the literal path we take toward recovery of our facial movement; it's about how we dig deep and find our true selves despite the hardships we endure. It's both literal and figurative and probably everything in between. These authors want you to feel supported as if they were your dear friend sharing and reminiscing about old times and new days ahead. Welcome to The Hunt for YOUR Smile!

· • • ● • ● • • ·

My hunt began the morning I woke with an earache that turned into a much scarier and more unknown beast over the course of three days. The pain in my ear didn't make sense, nothing would dampen the pain, and the noise entering my ear sounded like someone was holding a megaphone and screaming. The third morning I woke, and my face had begun to fall. True to form, being a solo mom on a Sunday morning, we were off to hockey, and I ignored the symptoms believing that it was related to the ear pain and would go away when the pain subsided. By the afternoon, my family was worried I had experienced a stroke, and I visited an urgent care where I was misdiagnosed with Bell's palsy. This visit probably saved me from more severe facial nerve damage because the doctor gave me a shot of steroids and a tapering dose of meds to take home and sent me on my way. But that was it; I was given no other instructions, mentions of treatment, or suggestions for care. I was on my own to figure out how to deal with my new reality.

Within two days of facial palsy onset, my eye was frozen open, my facial nerve was on fire, and I still didn't know where to get help. I had no blink, smile, or lift of my eyebrow. It was as if that side of my face just fell away and hid. By the third day after paralysis, I was fearful that it wasn't just Bell's palsy I was dealing with as my left ear was swollen like a red cauliflower. What was happening to me? "Dr. Google" diagnosed Ramsay Hunt syndrome, which occurs when your facial nerve is attacked by shingles, otherwise known as the herpes zoster oticus virus, that lies dormant in your body after you have had the chickenpox virus. A few days later, RHS was finally confirmed.

In the following weeks and months, the world shut down, so seeing a medical professional was impossible. I scoured the internet and found very few resources to help someone new to facial paralysis and finally found one in the summer of 2020 when the book *Fix My Face* was released. It was a medical resource published by the Foundation for Facial Recovery and my soon-to-be Physical Therapist, Jodi Barth, and partners. This book gives specific and detailed information for a layperson looking to help themselves through facial palsy. It was the first helpful literary resource I found, and I still refer to it over three years post-onset. It touches on all areas of concern, starting with getting medical treatment as soon as possible and going through stretches and exercises to help ease the aches and pain, loosen muscle tightness, and lessen the chance for synkinesis, a by-product of new nerve growth as healing begins. Synkinesis may be the worst side effect as it affects the movement of your eye, often causing it to be squinted and close on its own when you talk, eat, yawn, smile, laugh, or get tired.

I was in my eighth month of facial paralysis when I scheduled my first virtual consultation with Jodi. She helped me get a consult with Michael J. Reilly, MD, at MedStar Georgetown University, and he quickly saw the virus was still active in my swollen face. He was the *first* doctor to recommend and help me get on the one medication that would help quiet the virus: antivirals. He was also the first doctor who made me feel like he understood what I was going through, and I felt hopeful as I began to build a team of medical professionals to help me find my recovery. I took the antivirals for a year while I saw Jodi virtually every few weeks to work on facial exercises and stretching to improve the synkinesis and symmetry of my face. I eventually added Botox to help with the closing of my eye and the cramping of the platysma muscle in my neck.

I gained a step toward emotional healing during the summer of 2021 when I shared my story of RHS in *The Truth About Finding Joy in the Darkness*. If you've experienced facial paralysis, you understand that finding joy in the midst of losing your ability to smile, and communicate to the world how you are feeling with your face, isn't done without significant effort. Writing helped me in my recovery and it was one way I knew I could help others. Thus the idea of this book began.

• • • ● • ● ● • • •

Why call it *The Hunt for My Smile?* Simple. It's a play on words. I lost my smile due to Ramsay HUNT syndrome. When searching for something lost or hidden, like Easter eggs, you go on a HUNT. I was on a journey to discover who I was beyond my ability to smile. You see, throughout my life, I used my smile to hide. I hid from emotions, stressful situations, and uncomfortable encounters (ironically, this is likely why shingles raised its ugly head, attacking my facial nerve and causing the very thing that took my smile from me). I could slap a smile on my face and pretend all was ok. Once my face fell, half of my face drooped and wouldn't move even when I felt joyful and happy. The twinkle in my eye was dead, and the expression on my face was a big ol' ugly, grumpy frown that betrayed how I felt on the inside. It is a challenge to feel happy when you can't express happiness outwardly. Part of my journey to recovery has been the mental and emotional aspect of finding my smile – my happiness – my joy.

This book collaborative has given me purpose and fulfilled an innate need to be helpful in this life. Besides the birth of my two sons, this may be the most significant experience of my life because not only did I get to help twenty-three people share their stories, but by proxy, I got to experience their healing. I knew what was in store for them when they decided to put pen to paper or tap on the keys of their computer and voice how they navigated through their paralysis. I knew their stories would fill the pages and create a place for you, the reader, to connect with them. I knew this would help them feel heard. I knew this book would create a ripple effect and offer hope and inspiration for you to keep taking one step at a time, advocating for yourself and your health, and paving the way for the next wave of readers who find themselves lost without their smiles.

I have always loved my smile. I lost it a time or two before (due to other life stories) and promised myself I would never lose it again. But when you get facial paralysis, you don't have a choice. It is taken from you, and you may or may not get it back physically, but you *can* get it back emotionally and find ways to express how you feel. Your smile is more than the lips on your face curving upwards to a crescent moon shape. It is the twinkle in your eye and the energy that flows through you. It is also the thoughts in your head, the feelings in your heart, and the actions of your hands. Early on, I had it wrong, and it took me some time to realize that searching for an upturned curve on my face was not what I really desired. I wanted people to understand how I felt about them and convey my mental/emotional space. When I realized it was more than the symmetry of my face, I knew the hunt for my smile was no longer a journey somewhere outside but within me.

Now that we are friends and you have read my reason for creating this book, I invite you to continue the emotional journey of twenty-four brave and inspiring souls who share their experiences of living with facial paralysis and navigating the trials that come along with it. If you feel a strong connection to this community, hope for resilience, a desire to speak up and use your voice, or are inspired to write and share your story to help those who are beginning the hunt for their smile, then we have done our job. We are in this together.

-Amy Sameck

ABOUT THE AUTHOR

Amy Sameck is an author, publisher, solo mompreneur, teacher, and counselor who holds a Master's degree in Marriage and Family Counseling, Ed.S. from the University of Florida.

In November 2019, Amy learned she had Ramsay Hunt syndrome after several days of earache pain and left-side facial paralysis. Through her healing journey, she discovered her love for writing and helping others to uncover and share their stories which manifested as this book collaborative and creating a coaching program. In the fall of 2021, she authored a chapter in *The Truth About Finding Joy in the Darkness* book collaborative, and in the spring of 2022, she self-published the journal, *The Reminiscence Project*.

Amy is blessed with two amazing teenage sons, Taylor and Jonah, and their little girl pup, Megatron, who now rules the house. Her favorite place on earth is in the British Virgin Islands, and she believes she's meant to live on a boat in the Caribbean or the mountains of N. Carolina.

Connect with Amy at amy@amysameck.com.

Connect with Amy:

/amysameck

/amysameck

www.amysameck.com

1

Real Over Perfect

Barbie Wharton

Vancouver, BC, Canada

I never knew exactly what I wanted to be when I grew up. When I was a young girl, I said I would own my own business and have a beautiful office with a glass desk, and there would be a fridge in the corner with lots of chocolate milk. I can still see the image clearly in my mind. I would be a successful businesswoman and find a partner who would support me on any journey I wanted to take. Once I was an adult, I would be important. I just needed to get there.

On professional days from school, when other kids did "kid" things, I went to my Grandma's office and got to answer the phones, photocopy papers, and use office supplies. I knew I belonged there, and I felt like I mattered. When I was with other kids, I felt like I was an observer of the fun things happening. I never quite felt the same as everyone else; I felt like I was missing something or didn't belong there. I had a good childhood with very supportive and loving parents, but I was always making plans for when I was an adult. I had goals and dreams, and I achieved them.

By the time I was thirty-five, I was married and had two young, healthy, and happy boys. We lived in the perfect suburb and the perfect house. We were always surrounded by people; I threw fantastic parties, and from the outside, everything was – perfect. I had a successful career as an entrepreneur, working alongside my mom and sister, and yes, I even had a big office with a glass desk. I now know I am intolerant to dairy (which would have been handy to know back when I was 10!), so the chocolate milk wasn't there, but it could have been if I wanted it to be. I had created the perfect life I had set out to have as a young girl.

Here's the thing about "perfect" – it's not real. Perfect does not exist. It is an illusion you create from your observations of other people's lives throughout the years that you piece together to cultivate a vision of something you think is right for you. Your goals never seem to manifest in the exact way you think they will, and even if they do, the feeling is not exactly what you expected. That is because you never quite arrive at the "perfect" destination.

Somewhere along the line, you get so focused on the degree, the career, the wedding, and the house, that you don't notice the little signs along the way showing you other possible paths or opportunities. Or, you see them, but you silence the voice in your head telling you what you know is true because it is easier at the time to ignore it.

You know the voice. The one that tells you to speak up for yourself, say no, or change your opinion or focus. In the moment, it seems easier to keep the peace, take the blame that wasn't yours, or just agree so you don't make waves. You put everyone else first, please your parents or partner, and don't quit because you have already put so much into it. It's easier… until it isn't. The exact scenario doesn't matter. If this resonates with you, I get you.

When I woke up in 2015 with facial paralysis, I was not "shocked," which is what most people understandably assume. I wasn't worried I had had a stroke or a life-threatening illness. I was surprisingly calm and accepted it right away as a message from the Universe – a "smack across the face." I just had to figure out what the message was. No one really understood anything that I was going through, so I began reading about the metaphysical reasons for facial paralysis, and the message was loud and clear. *I was not using my voice.*

Your intuition will tell you what you need to hear if you are open to it. I was not using my voice, so my mouth stopped working. I have always been chatty, so it's pretty ironic, but talking is not the same as using your voice. I was not standing up for myself or standing in my light. There was more for me out there and more to me than I was honoring. It was time to listen to the Universe, figure out the messy stuff, and get to where I was meant to be.

I have learned many things over the past seven years since waking up with a paralyzed face. But the most important one is to speak your truth, be real even if it's messy and scary, and find people who understand you. It must be a priority to surround yourself with people who are real and who accept you as your authentic self. It is time to find new people if you feel small, judged, or alone when you are with them. It has been difficult for me to separate myself from many people who used to be in my life, but to make room for new things, we need to purge those that don't serve us anymore. The dress you bought on sale ten years ago that you always meant to wear is one of those things. And so are the people who do not see you for you, forgive you as you have forgiven them, or make you a priority in some way. When you let go of those attachments, you make room for new dresses, new support systems, and new places to wear outfits you bought in this decade.

In 2020, we made the heartbreaking decision to close our family business, which ended my lifelong dream. Afterward, a friend suggested I start a community for people with Bell's palsy to use my voice and share my journey. So, I made *Bell's Palsy Talk*. Initially, I thought it would be a place to talk about treatments and experiences, but it has turned into much more than that. It is a place for others to share and be heard. Together, we feel understood and valued because we have all been through something life-changing that no one else really "gets." Being understood is vital for every human being, regardless of the issue, whether it is facial paralysis, weight loss, addiction, trauma, or anything in your life. Coming together with people who understand and honor you is the only way to begin healing anything.

If you come to visit me, I do not want you to pretend you are perfect. That's boring anyway. I want you to feel like you can tell me your favorite story three times, laugh until you cry, and make a mess in my kitchen making tea or pouring yourself a glass of wine. You do not need to pretend, and I will not judge. I will always be grateful to my friend Ashley for encouraging me to use my voice and to create the *Bell's Palsy Talk* community. I am also proud of myself for being brave because while having a community helps us all, giving others a safe place to use their voice and learn that they truly matter is healing for me, too. It is a gift to bring others together and make a difference in their lives and journeys.

While I still have places to go, I have found a place where my smile is finally back. I no longer strive for perfection or have goals or destinations that are set in stone. I try to care about something other than proving myself or keeping up with the illusions. I try not to pay attention to the voices telling me I am not enough. I focus on being present and grateful for where I am now and my opportunities to grow and expand in this life. I have also found my true love now, and I feel no ceiling and no expectations from him other than to be my authentic self. The only rules we have are to be honest and real at all times. I speak my mind and heart, and it gets messy sometimes (actually, a lot of the time). But it is never easier to be silent, paralyzed.

Your voice matters. You are real, and you are important.

ABOUT THE AUTHOR

Barbie Wharton is an author, speaker, and Bell's palsy advocate known for her infectious passion and continuous resilience. She leads a community called "Bell's Palsy Talk with Barbie" on Facebook and Instagram, encouraging her followers and those affected by facial paralysis to come together. The focus is on self-compassion while learning their true purpose in a safe and inclusive space. She is also a successful entrepreneur and management consultant.

In 2015, she was struck with paralysis on the left side of her face and has since focused on learning self-care and stepping into her light. She also began advocating for those with facial paralysis using her talent and interviewing others to spread awareness. She is passionate about making people feel like they belong and that their voice matters. This book is the first step in creating opportunities for people to come together and create inspirational stories while helping each other in their healing journeys.

She enjoys watching her two teenage sons play lacrosse with her husband, Trevor, and their puppy, Cherry.

You can find more information on Barbie and her projects at www.barbiewharton.com.

Connect with Barbie:

 /bellspalsytalk

 /bellspalsytalk

 /@BellsPalsyTalk

 www.barbiewharton.com

2

Returning to Life after RHS

Ilan Livne

Haifa, Isreal

My story began in March 2018, when I moved to Haifa, a city located in the north part of Israel, where I was about to start a Ph.D. program. I was excited about starting my new academic journey in a new city where I was hoping to meet new people and create new friendships. After two months, in May 2018, everything suddenly stopped: I was misdiagnosed with Bell's palsy after having ear pain and facial weakness, while, in fact, I had Ramsay Hunt syndrome (RHS). The doctor at the ER prescribed a twelve-day course of steroids and sent me home while mentioning that the chances of recovery were over 90%. Since I had some friends who were also doctors, I asked for their opinion about my diagnosis and recommended medical treatment. They all agreed I should be fine since I got the steroids early on.

After a few days, I started to feel ringing in my ears, and a little rash appeared in my ear. I went to a follow-up consultation with my primary doctor, and he immediately put me on an antiviral medication, which he mentioned I should have taken right from the beginning. He also mentioned that the virus could replicate itself very quickly, and the antiviral drug helped stop this fast replication.

On my last day of steroids, I started to feel extreme ear pain. I went back to the ER, but since my medical record showed that my diagnosis was "just" Bell's palsy, no one took my complaints about extreme ear pain too seriously. After a few hours of waiting in extreme pain, a doctor eventually saw me and sent me home without any new insight. I was released home with pain relief pills and told to "hope for the best."

By this time, my face was completely paralyzed, my ear was ringing, and my eye was burning and itching so much that I had to tape it down. As the weeks passed and I did not see any improvement, I became very worried. My life completely stopped. I could not work on my research. I skipped university classes. I was suffering from severe eye pain and depression. I realized I needed help, so I moved home to live with my mom.

I needed help to understand what was happening to my life. The girl I had started dating a few weeks before the palsy hit left me during this time. Within a few weeks, I went from an energetic, happy person who was excited about his new life to a suffering person, depressed without any energy. A neurologist told me I was the worst case he had ever seen. The future seemed dark. There were days I stayed in my bed until 5:00 p.m., refusing to accept the new reality. My mind went over and over the chain of events before and after the diagnosis. I tried to understand what I did wrong to deserve this nightmare. I repeatedly imagined alternative realities where I would get the antivirals within the important 72-hour window, an imaginary path that hopefully led to complete recovery.[1] I was devastated and defeated.

After eleven to twelve weeks of complete palsy on the right side of my face, I started to see the first movement. During this time, I also started researching what I was dealing with online. I learned that about 15% of people with Bell's palsy suffer from a severe nerve injury called Axonotmesis,[2] while the other 85% suffer from a mild nerve injury called Neuropraxia.[3] Axonotmesis means the nerve wires are crushed severely and degenerate in a well-known process called Wallerian Degeneration.[4] After this degeneration occurs, the nerve must regrow again until it re-connects to the muscles. On the contrary, those suffering from mild nerve damage typically do not experience this complete degeneration process, and their original nerve fully recovers. I continued my research and learned that those with a severe nerve injury, such as mine, typically experience a delayed recovery which means that the first facial movement only starts after three to four months. Their recovery path includes three well-known stages: flaccid,[5] paresis,[6] and synkinesis.[7] I was astonished that no doctor I met made an effort to explain all this to me.

I started physical therapy (PT) that was offered to me by standard insurance care. Unfortunately, the PT who treated me was not a specialist in this field, and she used inappropriate practices such as gross exercises, forcing strong movements, and electrical stimulation [8] therapy. Later in my journey, I learned that facial nerve experts agree that these practices can increase the likelihood of developing synkinesis and are not recommended. After a few months, my doctor referred me to a special synkinesis clinic, "merely" a ninety-minute drive away from where

I lived. I was excited to know I would finally be treated by specialists who really understood this area. Sadly, it didn't take more than half an hour to realize that this "specialist's" level of understanding was extremely low. They tried to convince me that the tension and pain in my platysma muscle[9] (neck area) had nothing to do with my facial palsy or synkinesis. They insisted that the platysma muscle was not innervated by the facial muscle, which is an extremely embarrassing mistake. At that point, I finally realized that I wouldn't be able to find the help I needed within the borders of Israel. I searched for international specialists overseas and found Jackie Diels,[10] a worldwide expert in synkinesis and nerve injury rehabilitation. After the first session with Jackie, I finally knew that I was in the right hands to start my rehab journey. This journey is still ongoing today and has also included three different surgeries (platinum weight, DAO resection,[11] and platysma resection[12]) and Botox injections every few months.

As to my professional life, it took me about five months to get back on my feet and leave my mom's house. I returned to the city of Haifa, where my university was located, and continued my Ph.D. journey again. I rented a new apartment. I did not want to return to the old apartment where the paralysis hit me. I was traumatized. I wanted to put all of it behind me and start fresh again. But I was not the same person. Something profound in this experience changed the way I saw myself and the way I saw the world. I lost my optimistic view of the world. The injustice of this experience brought with it a deep understanding that life can be ever so fragile, and everything can completely change in a second. This experience changed me forever. In addition, with my face moving unintentionally with every blink due to chronic synkinesis, it was impossible for me to "forget about it and move on." The residuals of this physical and psychological trauma were always with me. I had constant eye pain, making it almost impossible to concentrate on my research as before. I became a weak and pale shadow of myself. People kept telling me, "I can't even see it," not realizing that they also couldn't see the facial expressions that would have existed had I not suffered from facial palsy. People were trying to be nice but did not realize that, in most cases, they unintentionally did what is known as _toxic positivity_,[13] which made me feel worse.

—

In the following, I will try to concisely share with you another side of my facial palsy story: my journey as an advocate for the facial palsy community in Israel.

After being let down by the medical community in Israel, I became angry. Very angry. I wanted to take revenge for what happened to me. I felt like my life was ruined, and no one cared. I became angrier when I realized that my experience was not unique. The personal stories of other people from the facial palsy community made it clear that it was very common to be misdiagnosed by doctors and treated wrongly by therapists who were ignorant about facial palsy. The correlation-causation confusion[14] affected almost all non-specialist therapists, making them believe they were successfully helping patients. Instead, their treatment kept perpetuating the wrong and harmful treatments. I was angry about the gap between research and practice, which revealed that experienced nerve experts treat patients completely differently[15] than inexperienced doctors who just follow the current medical protocol. During this time, I also created a Facebook support

group for people from Israel who suffered from facial palsy and shared
everything I learned about this topic. In addition, I collaborated with
Cristina Toso, a facial palsy warrior and advocate, who is a fellow author
of this book. Together we built the Facial-Paralysis Information Bot[16]
to help other people. Believing in my ability to create a change in this
field, I took the next step and contacted the top universities in Israel
responsible for PT training. I explained that their lack of knowledge and
understanding was hurting people and that they needed to change their
curriculum as soon as possible. Almost all the universities ignored me,
but one did call me back and listened to what I had to say. From that
point, things started to roll. Mara Robinson,[17] a specialist in this field,
and the Haifa university in Israel collaborated. Mara gave a workshop
to over 180 physical therapists in Israel, educating them about what
to do and what to avoid when treating facial palsy patients. Soon
after her workshop, a new guideline was published within the Israeli
physical therapy community, which ended the inappropriate practices
such as electrical stimulation and forcing gross facial expressions while
ignoring the different stages of recovery and the different types of
nerve damage[18] that are common in Bell's palsy. I received emails from
therapists who apologized for the bad-practice treatments they used
over the years. Fortunately, following Mara Robinson's workshop, a few
enthusiastic Israeli therapists contacted worldwide specialists, such as
Catriona Neville,[19] to learn more in-depth skills and qualifications in facial
palsy rehabilitation.[20] These therapists basically "imported" to Israel the
best practices and educated their colleagues. I was proud and happy to
see the ongoing change, but at the same time, I knew that the biggest

challenge would be to create a change in how doctors [mis]diagnose and treat patients.

At this point in my advocacy journey, I created a Facebook group that grew to over a thousand people. Among them were doctors and a nurse who were also affected by facial palsy. We became a team, and today we work together to improve the way patients are diagnosed and treated in Israel. To ensure that RHS, or any other cause, was not missed and that the right medication was properly prescribed, when a newly diagnosed person joins my Facebook group, he is immediately referred to a specialist that is available within a few hours, free of charge!! We are currently working to promote a new guideline that will hopefully reduce the huge variation in diagnosis and treatment that exists today among different doctors who treat BP and RHS patients.

To learn more about my work, feel free to visit my facial-palsy website (Hebrew language): https://facial-paralysis.org.il/[21]

---

1. Antivirals does not guarantee complete recovery. There are many people who were treated by antivirals withing 72 hours window that did not fully recover.
2. https://en.wikipedia.org/wiki/Axonotmesis
3. For RHS the likelihood of axonotmesis is even higher than for BP.
4. https://en.wikipedia.org/wiki/Wallerian_degeneration?fbclid=IwAR1 5COVllCJyPsuo8ZkBJc0luVReHN0h33UanjySIZRYsUzhRAImMwESJzw
5. https://www.facialpalsy.org.uk/support/self-help-videos/managem ent-of-flaccid-facial-paralysis-floppy-face/?fbclid=IwAR3oyK5Mu1F9 OxBkHSz4bkAvylserJiD36F5wjl0PKGjO8BZ6HSRRBrH2Sc

6. https://www.facialpalsy.org.uk/support/self-help-videos/managem ent-of-paresis/?fbclid=IwAR10pgCol4z_eU4fW4S7-o-Pn_dCowOyYjT eio_69HJz45MhlsTLiEj0pVs

7. https://www.facialpalsy.org.uk/support/self-help-videos/managem ent-of-synkinesis-tight-face/?fbclid=IwAR1nknizkVzoFaClDLs4KmEk 68l9xHn73WyxbLmL97Qi5oVxsc6NkFJ14k0

8. https://www.facialpalsy.org.uk/support/treatments-therapies/elect rical-stimulation/?fbclid=IwAR3uHvOAqZtnp7g08wtDdcU8Ku7wmo pxh7Y6wbc_m-82VoSOTzjOSclJ0PE

9. https://en.wikipedia.org/wiki/Platysma_muscle

10. https://www.facialretraining.com/

11. https://www.facialnervecenter.org/depressor-anguli-oris-dao-excisi on

12. https://pubmed.ncbi.nlm.nih.gov/21768558/

13. https://www.verywellmind.com/what-is-toxic-positivity-5093958

14. https://www.youtube.com/watch?v=RmmnCA_76QE

15. https://www.youtube.com/watch?v=HFhjy6QOEKg

16. https://m.me/110403753934092

17. https://www.facialnervecenter.org/mara-robinson

18. https://www.facialpalsy.org.uk/support/patient-guides/facial-nerve- injury-the-three-types-of-injury/?fbclid=IwAR2Lr3BE8UtLUIcbodVZF ss0nk4NU5XutL9vvQDecRD2aJ81p1treAUin7o

19. https://www.youtube.com/watch?v=i_4VAfs-uds

20. https://facialtherapyspecialists.com/ftsi-practical-and-advanced-co urses/

21. https://facial-paralysis.org.il/

ABOUT THE AUTHOR

Ilan Livne is a statistician and holds a Ph.D. in statistics from The
Technion, Israel Institute of Technology. He tries to raise awareness and
improve treatments for those affected by facial palsy. He is a dedicated
advocate for the facial palsy community in Israel and proudly plays a role
in advancing the healthcare system in Israel by communicating the
importance of receiving a proper diagnosis, medical treatment, and
physical therapy.

After personally experiencing the effects of Ramsay Hunt syndrome in
2018, Ilan founded and currently serves as the administrator of a support
group for individuals dealing with facial palsy in Israel. He also developed
a bot that assists users in finding support and expert advice on managing
facial palsy. Ilan has shared his story in this book with the hope that it can
provide guidance and support to others facing facial palsy.

Ilan is married to his lovely wife and is a father of baby twins. He enjoys
running, hiking, and helping people in the facial-palsy community.

Connect with Ilan on his facial palsy (Hebrew) website:
www.facial-paralysis.org.il.

Connect with Ilan:

 /ilan.livne

 www.facial-paralysis.org.il/

Scan Here
for access to the
Facial Paralysis Talks
Informational Bot

3

Mirror, Mirror on the Wall

Angel Faulk

Nashville, TN, USA

After three days in the ICU, I finally felt strong enough and brave enough to walk to the bathroom alone for the first time since brain surgery. As I very slowly approached the bathroom doorway, I paused, remembering there was a mirror just inches above the sink. I realized I could look at my face for the first time since surgery, but was I ready?

Just a few months before the surgery, an MRI discovered a tumor growing on my brain stem. The doctors were amazed that I could still balance, teach fitness classes, and lead an active life with my husband, Wade, and children, Lydia and Ethan. At the time, my only symptom was losing hearing on the right side. However, losing my hearing was a gift because that is what ended up saving my life.

After the MRI, getting an appointment with a surgeon specializing in brain tumors was challenging. Dr. David Haynes was a highly recommended and well-respected neurosurgeon, and I chose him as my surgeon. At my initial consult, he discussed the details of the surgery. As he explained the dangers of the surgery with his hands and held his fingers together, saying it's "like a game of pick-up sticks," I noticed he was missing parts of his fingers.

Upon this realization, I no longer heard anything he was saying. It was as if Charlie Brown's teacher was speaking at the head of the class, "wah waah wah waah wah waah!" I wondered how a man with nubs for fingers could do brain surgery. Later, when my senses returned to me, and Dr. Haynes had left the room, Wade and I discussed his missing fingers. The nurse explained that despite missing parts of his fingers, he was a top-notch surgeon, one of the very best. We knew God had placed me with the right doctor and were confident in this surgeon. He also provided Dr. Reid Thompson to assist in the surgery; he was the head of brain tumor research and neurosurgery at Vanderbilt University.

Dr. Thompson showed me the scans of my brain and explained I might not be able to teach my fitness classes or live my life as usual for up to a year and a half. He suggested I get my life in order and schedule surgery within the next three months. I had to make many hard sacrifices and decisions, and I admit I was very nervous. But overall, I felt like I was in good hands at Vanderbilt Medical Center in Nashville, and through prayer and the support of my Bible study, family, friends, and neighbors, I knew it would be ok.

The surgeons explained that it would be a long and tedious surgery because the meningioma tumor was quite large and looked like it had been growing for ten years. It was oddly shaped, with tails growing into the nerves of my brainstem, making it very difficult to pick apart and remove without causing severe damage.

After the grueling, fourteen-hour surgery, the doctors told me that my facial nerve was still intact, but it was severely stretched due to the tumor size and had collapsed when they removed the tumor. This damage caused facial paralysis. I wasn't sure what I would look like, they didn't know how long it would last or how severe the damage was, and no one knew how it would affect my daily life.

They also told me if I had not had the surgery, I might have died in my sleep. This news was a terrifying shock because I had visited an ENT about some hearing loss just a few years before and was told, "just keep an eye on it." He wasn't concerned, so I trusted his advice. Now, I regret not being proactive, asking more questions, and finding the cause of my hearing loss. Looking back, if I had received an MRI and surgery three years earlier, I might still have some hearing, and I might still have my smile.

Standing in the ICU bathroom, I looked in the mirror, prepared to see my partially paralyzed face. As I stared at the reflection of my face, my first thought was a prayer to God, "We're going on another adventure." I knew I wasn't alone, and this didn't surprise Him. I knew that with God in my life, I could face anything. He was my strength! A sense of supernatural peace came over me, and I said, "I'm ready. Let's go." I knew I would be ok because He was with me. I had overcome much in my life, clinging to God and His strength, and I knew I would somehow overcome this, too.

Having facial paralysis is uncomfortable physically, but the deeper pain is emotional. I don't feel pretty, and it often feels like people pity or misjudge me. My new norm leaves me feeling that I must explain myself during every first encounter with a new friend. I have tried many treatments, such as Botox. It is supposed to help with the synkinesis and pulling in the neck area, but only one session out of four worked well for me. One particular botox treatment left me looking permanently worse. Facial physical therapy worked initially, but my progress plateaued, and I stopped going. When I try to smile and hide my paralysis or look as symmetrical as possible, it ends up looking fake, making me look angry or unhappy. I would love to naturally smile again, showing all my teeth, free and happy, without thinking about it!

Living in the past doesn't change what happened, so I choose to look forward and use my story to help others. I have moments when I miss my smile, but I practice gratitude daily to help me through those moments. I focus on what I *can* do, reminding myself who I am in Christ and all I have overcome. This focus keeps me going, especially on the hard days. This is me -- the good, the not-so-perfect, real, authentic me!

Turning my pain into purpose by helping others also keeps me going. I teach lifestyle habits that prevent, reverse, and fight sickness and disease. I inspire healthy living around the world! We only get one body, and we have been given the ability to choose health and joy! It's my mission to help others do this.

At the time of my surgery, my Bible study group was studying faith and working through the book of Hebrews. At the next Bible study session, we worshiped at the altar and sang a new song called "Healer" by Kari Jobe. The worship leader did not know this song had become my anthem, and someone had given me the CD the week before. With my eyes closed and my hands lifted, I felt the Lord speak to my heart. He told me two things:

1. Your faith has made you whole.
2. You will be pleasantly surprised.

I wrote those promises in my study Bible, knowing I would cling to these words in my healing journey and it would be part of my testimony. It's essential to record the important moments in life.

God has blessed me more than I could have asked or imagined. Living with facial paralysis isn't what I would have chosen, but the relationships I've made through this experience have brought me so much joy! The special moments and lessons I've learned through the trials have made me stronger, and I've also become more compassionate and a whole lot more patient.

My brain tumor led me to research health and eventually start a wellness franchise, impacting thousands of lives I wouldn't have otherwise. I was the ambassador for Nashville's Brain Tumor 5K, and I have an annual Dance Party in May, Brain Tumor Awareness Month, giving all donations to Brain Tumor Research at Vanderbilt. God turned my tragedy into triumph, and I believe He will do it for you too!

Please reach out to me for prayer, support, or help on your health journey.

ABOUT THE AUTHOR

Angel Faulk has been married thirty years to her husband, Wade, and they are the proud parents of Ethan, Lydia, and son-in-law, Jonah. She has a degree in education but followed her passion as a health and nutrition expert. Nicknamed the "Fitness Angel," she's created Christian fitness DVDs and has flourished as a businesswoman, coach, and speaker. Her passion for research on health and longevity led her to a successful global health company where she has helped many attain healthy lifestyle habits.

At forty, a brain tumor caused facial paralysis, single-sided deafness, and other health issues, but she doesn't let this stop her from fully living life. Angel's heart for sharing her story stems from memories of what it was like in the early days of paralysis. She searched for literary resources for support and desired to connect with others like her. God turned her pain into purpose, and she hopes to inspire others to pursue their passion.

Angel enjoys speaking for women's groups and churches, sharing her testimony, teaching what she has learned about faith, fitness, and health, and leading PRAISE parties!

Connect with Angel at angelfaulk2@gmail.com.

Connect with Angel:

[Instagram] /thefitnessangel

[Facebook] /TheZumbangel

[Web] www.afaulk.juiceplus.com/us/en

[*] /thefitnessangel

4

Symmetry is Overrated

Renee Hacker

Rockton, IL, USA

W ho would have thought that facial palsy could bring me acceptance and confidence? I guess you *can* teach an old dog new tricks.

I developed Bell's palsy in February 2020 during a vacation in Florida and was told (as most of us are) that I would recover quickly. The ear pain and headaches in the first three weeks gave way to "just" the fallen face. I felt like the right side of my face had melted off and was resting on my shoulder. Eating and drinking were difficult, and eye gel became my constant companion. "I can deal with this; it's temporary, right?"

My first trip out to dinner was memorable. What would I eat in public? I had to hold my lips out of the way to take a bite of anything as they would collapse into my mouth. Liquid would just run out. I could feel it escaping but was helpless to stop it. Soup was the best choice. There was nothing to bite, and I could easily spoon it in a little at a time with one hand. Meanwhile, I was awkwardly holding a napkin to my lips with the other hand to catch the cascade that involuntarily exited my mouth.

Sitting behind my husband was an elderly lady, and we had a direct line of vision with each other. She had noticed my melted face, but she mostly went about a conversation with her dinner companion with small glances my way now and then. The soup was served, and it looked delicious! I sat with a spoon in one hand and a napkin in the other – the soup tasted great, but as expected, it dribbled out the corner of my mouth. The napkin was there to quickly catch any escaping soup, and I felt triumphant until I looked up and saw the horrified look on the elderly lady's face. I don't know if it was revulsion or pity; frankly, it didn't matter. She looked at me differently than I ever had been looked at in my life, and I didn't like it. Here was a woman in her 70's, and I was 59, yet I was the one feeling old and broken.

We returned to northern Illinois the first week of March, tanned and, for the most part, relaxed. This fallen face was temporary, after all. It felt comforting to be home, yet I was back in the real world. My new real world, but the only thing new was that my face had fallen. Everything else was still the same. Then it was time to head to the grocery store, the first real-world task since returning from Florida. I told myself it should be a piece of cake, that I could do this.

I've always been on the taller side with a long reach, and because of this, I would often get asked for help to reach something on a top shelf. Strangers were at ease with me when they saw my smile and felt comfortable approaching me. Let's make that past tense. That first trip to the grocery store made it clear that my approachable and friendly face was gone. I unconsciously tried to smile at people in the aisles, but it was heartbreakingly mistaken for a grimace. Here I was, once again, being looked at differently. I felt the same inside and sometimes even forgot about my lopsided face. I wanted to shout, "I'm me! I'm still the same!" Then I got a reprieve two weeks later when Covid locked everything down.

By late spring 2020, we were able to be outside again. We stayed six feet apart, but I felt very vulnerable with no mask. Meeting with friends and family who hadn't seen me was almost like meeting for the first time; a bit of anxiety mixed with knowing deep down that I was accepted. Still me! By the middle of summer, it seemed like my face was getting a little better. It wasn't hanging in the loose way it had been, and I felt very hopeful. I thought, maybe it *is* temporary, just like they said! I enjoyed a couple of weeks filled with this hope, but that hope ended when I noticed that my mouth was pulling — uncomfortably. My cheek was hard as a rock, and my eye jumped in on every move my mouth made. Oh boy, now what?

As the flaccid paralysis of Bell's palsy gave way to the tight and spasming new world of synkinesis, my attitude was changing, too. This was the new me, and it was here to stay. I visited the Facial Nerve Clinic at the University of Wisconsin at Madison Hospital. The diagnosis of severe synkinesis was confirmed, and though they could help, my big, wide, toothy smile was gone. My right eye would always be smaller than the left. I had to let that sink in. I had continued to be hopeful that somehow, some way, my former face would return. After a day of cussing and crying, I felt acceptance. I would start Botox and facial retraining in the fall.

I always felt accepted by family and friends. My husband made me feel secure in my new look, telling me that I was still beautiful – just in a different way. I've always had a sense of humor, and it was coming to my rescue now. I could joke about my one-eyed pirate look while drinking Captain Morgan rum. I'd never had a poker face, but now people could not read me, so time to go to Vegas, baby! Speaking of Vegas, I could only lift my lip on one side: maybe an Elvis impersonator? Thank you, thank you very much.

I was also starting to develop a can-do attitude. I had to advocate for myself with my insurance company. They wanted to see my procedures as cosmetic instead of restorative. Functionality was the only thing that mattered, and I was determined that they would not deny me medical care for a medical issue. I dug in my heels, researched, and reached out to people who could help. Frustration turned to confidence. What doesn't kill us makes us stronger, and these battles with insurance made me much stronger.

Having something to fight for was the motivation I needed, and in the end, learning to navigate the insurance world brought me great satisfaction. I'd spent my entire adult life in dental offices and dealing with dental insurance; I used that experience to assist me here. There are three specific things to know when dealing with insurance:

- Don't be intimidated. The customer service number on your insurance card is there for YOU. Use it! Call and ask as many questions as you need. Remember that the representatives that answer the phone have no medical experience. They can answer basic questions regarding your plan but nothing more. Ask to speak with a supervisor or someone in the medical review department for explanations of why a procedure is in question or being denied. Always ask for the person's name and the encounter number. Each and every phone call on their end must be documented.

- Keep open communication with your medical team's insurance department. Have their name and extension handy; help them to help you. They need to send what is called a "narrative" along with insurance claims and medical codes explaining in detail why they need to do a certain procedure. Don't hold back on your symptoms. They need this information for maximum coverage.

- Lean on your human resource department or whoever is in charge of your medical insurance. They can help you communicate with the insurance company they have contracted. In my case, my insurance was self-insured, meaning the employer made the rules for coverage. Make sure that they understand that the procedures are not for cosmetic reasons but for restorative and functionality purposes.

Standing up for myself against the insurance company did something to change me. I no longer felt "less than." I continued to adjust to my new reality and discovered I was a fan of cubism art and the way asymmetry is seen as beautiful. I was seeing things through a new lens and liked what I saw. I'm a good person with a big heart, and if you can't see past my uniquely unique smile and squinty eye, then ... forget you!

This journey has taught me more about myself than I ever expected. The realization of the strength I had within me was huge. I walk with an air of self-confidence that I never had when I was younger and symmetrical.

I've learned that I can stand up for myself, and in doing so, I can now help others to do the same. Through it all, I have found a new identity:

"With age comes wisdom, with asymmetry comes fierceness." – Renee

ABOUT THE AUTHOR

Renee Hacker was born, raised, and continues to live in the Rockton, IL area. Recently retired, Renee spent her career in the dental field as an oral surgery assistant and front office coordinator.

On February 2, 2020, Renee's journey with facial paralysis began with Bell's palsy. Her experiences in social media groups and watching others struggle with wanting to hide from the world, coupled with her natural instinct to help others, inspired her to venture into writing. Renee hopes her insight with self-acceptance inspires others with facial palsy. Her professional experience with today's insurance system is invaluable in helping others navigate the daunting experience of facial palsy.

Renee and her husband have two adult children and are excitedly welcoming grandchildren to the growing family. Spending time at their lake cabin in Wisconsin, reading, and baking are activities she enjoys in her leisure time, not to mention spoiling their rescue mutt, Sofie.

Renee is an advocate for facial palsy and is always willing to help.

You can reach Renee at hacker.renee@gmail.com.

Connect with Renee:

✉ hacker.renee@gmail.com

5

The Struggles of Synkinesia in the 6th Grade

Terry Fox

Windsor, CO, USA

M oving from a rural country school to a proper town school was tough. It felt miraculous that I made it through the 5th grade. Despite the initial bullies, I'd made a lot of new friends. When school ended that year, the feeling of isolation was palpable. As the summer of 1987 progressed, my excitement to start 6th grade and reunite with my friends was rising. Or at least it was, until the morning when the right side of my face suddenly stopped working.

There are several theories about the cause of Bell's palsy. For me, it was likely due to a baseball injury. To this day, I wish I had caught that pop fly with my glove instead of my eye socket. Feeling time slow down, hearing the wincing exclamations emanate from the parental congregation in the bleachers, and the booming voice of the opposing team's coach yelling, "Keep rubbing it!" was a singularly unique sensation. The embarrassment of having all those eyes witness my spectacular failure filled my mind, and

I was mortified as the umpire stopped the game until I was led off into the dugout. Humiliation, burning my cheeks and ears, competed with the pain and swelling of an instantly blackened eye. That was the beginning. Three days later, Bell's palsy appeared.

As summer dwindled and my face persisted in its asymmetry, I began to dread the start of 6th grade. Wanting only to fit in, yet certain I couldn't, I knew I was screwed.

Wyoming folks tend to be pretty stoic. That's just part of cowboy culture. I wasn't supposed to cry or show weakness. All I could do was go to school and "Cowboy Up." So, I girded my loins, grabbed my backpack, put on my sunglasses, and armored my heart.

The twenty-mile school bus ride got underway with an initial barrage of stares, whispers, and outright insults. I endured it silently like the sad hobo clown at our local Fair and Rodeo parade. Stepping off the bus, it only got worse. I looked abnormal. And the others made sure it didn't slip my mind. I kept my sunglasses on, hoping they would help me look at least a little bit cool. The Goni twins sauntered up, identical smirks on their delinquent faces.

"Hey, F@**#t," one of them sneered. "Who are you supposed to be? Ray Charles?"

Some old "friends" from last year joined in on the ridicule. Their laughter stung in my ears; I had never experienced betrayal. This new kind of hurt sent a searing ache in my chest.

To the Yin of false friends was the Yang of Mark and Jared. They were my best buddies from 5th grade. I was overjoyed when, despite the others, they sat with me in the cafeteria. As I drank from the cardboard milk carton with the functional corner of my mouth, Mark cracked jokes to get me to laugh. And Jared said, "Just ignore those jerks." It was fraternal fidelity at its finest. I wasn't alone. At that moment, I learned what true friendship is. And even now, several decades later, I'm still grateful for their kindness.

During 5th grade, I started learning how to play the trombone. I loved it! The feel of the cool brass on my fingertips, the earthy aroma of slide oil, learning to read music and actually understanding it, and expressing myself through my instrument were all so good. To be succinct, Band was my favorite class. Until that year.

Now my lips wouldn't form correctly. Try as I might, I couldn't make the right vibrations into the mouthpiece. Yet again, I found myself hurled into public humiliation via Chair Challenges. Like a mallard duck with cemented feet, I'd be sunk to the bottom of the pecking order. For the challenge, all trombone players performed a pre-selected piece behind a curtain, and the rest of the band members voted on who sounded the best. Chair ranking was determined by who had the most votes.

I slowly shook my head as I listened to the other trombones play. In the depths of my chest, my heart began a loud and foreign beat of its own. I knew I would have to perform with all the other students listening intently and passing judgment. Despite the desperate prayers I quickly sent to the Almighty, my lips absolutely refused to do what they needed to do. My turn came. I took the brass handles in my sweating palms and gently placed my defective lips on the mouthpiece. The room was silent. I took a breath and gave it hell.

Valiantly playing the first half a dozen notes, the ugly truth was clear. I could have played better if I had put the mouthpiece to my butt cheeks. I knew it. And I knew everyone else knew it. So, instead of continuing the farce, I put down my trombone, swallowed hard, and stepped around the curtain. With all the band students looking on, feeling tears burning the corners of my eyes, I cleared my throat.

"Mrs. Phillips, I can't finish. May I just take Last Chair?" Hearing those words stumble out of my flaccid mouth was appalling.

She nodded. And I dejectedly took my seat, face flushed and feeling sick in my heart. At that moment, I despised myself and hated my music teacher for putting me in that situation. And I reviled everyone for witnessing my epic failure and complete embarrassment. As Band class ended and we shuffled out into the hallway, the sniggering comments I could hear behind my back added insult to injury.

For the majority of 6th grade, I did my best to hide away. Bullies do what they do. It was hard for me not to buy into the mean things they would say. A quiet terror began to germinate in the corners of my psyche. Fear of others, of myself, of my future. Would my face always be this way? How was I supposed to get a girl to look at me, let alone like me? How would I get a job when there are normal-looking people around? Would I be the Elephant Man of Wyoming? I couldn't bear looking at myself in the mirror. I worried my smile might never come back.

Praise be to the benevolent Lord. After several weeks, the palsy symptoms ploddingly began to recede. My eye started to close on its own again. The elation that came with blinking was glorious. The majority of my facial muscles slowly started regaining strength. And tentatively, I began to peek at the mirror. Good friends and solid family support allowed me to come out of my shell. Gradually, I did, but it took a few years.

To this day, I still have residual muscle weakness in my face. I have a hell of a time blowing up balloons. My children love watching me struggle at it, though! My right eye droops and squints more than the left, especially when I'm tired. Random muscle spasms on the right side of the face continue on a weekly, if not daily, basis. And I still have self-esteem struggles. It's difficult not to scrutinize photos. Public speaking and networking events challenge my desire to remain secluded and unseen. But I go and do them anyway.

I've discovered that life often puts challenges in front of us so that we might learn to serve others. In 2006, I earned my Master's Degree in Traditional Chinese Medicine. Acupuncture and Chinese herbs can reduce neural inflammation, increase circulation, and stimulate sagging muscles. It's an effective modality to support recovery from Bell's palsy and other facial nerve conditions. As a Licensed Acupuncturist, I've become an expert in Aesthetic and Facial Acupuncture.

No one should feel like I did about myself back then – afraid, despondent, and full of self-loathing. Through ancient wisdom and modern techniques, I now help others better their relationship with that amazing person they see in the mirror. I get to soothe fears and help folks find hope for their future. Witnessing a patient's recovery during their facial palsy journey brings me joy. Helping someone find their smile again is what helps me find mine!

ABOUT THE AUTHOR

Terry Fox, LMT, L.Ac., is Northern Colorado's Holistic Health and Beauty expert. He earned his Master's Degree from the Colorado School of Traditional Chinese Medicine. And in 2006, he founded Fox Haven Aesthetics. His focus is helping patients reclaim their authentic softness and radiance without resorting to toxins, fillers, or plastic surgery.

Terry was diagnosed with Bell's palsy after a baseball injury at age ten. He has aspired to be an author for many years. So, when given this opportunity, he decided to share his story. He hopes that others living with facial paralysis will feel encouraged to find their silver lining and never feel that life is limited.

Outside of the office, you can find Terry relaxing with his wife and two boys. He's an avid Sci-Fi and Fantasy fan. He crafts his own beer, wine, and liqueurs and occasionally competes in beard and mustache competitions.

Connect with Terry at www.foxhavenaethetics.com.

Connect with Terry:

 /FoxHavenAcu

 /FoxHavenAcu

 @FoxHavenAcu

 foxhavenaesthetics.com

6

Permission to F.L.Y.

Roshawn Dorsey

College Park, GA, USA

*D*ear Reader, allow me to share a little about myself before we start. My passion became a reality for ten years when I owned a dance studio. However, a broken neck, ruptured discs in my lower back from a couple of car accidents, and botched surgeries caused me to close my beloved school. I opened a dancewear boutique and later started a non-profit organization called Permission To F.L.Y.- Fully Love Yourself. I am also a mom to two beautiful queens and grandmother to two snookums.

Let me ask you a question. What is the word you use to describe being knocked down at your core, but you must keep going? I know that God creates thru my imagination, and I created a new word for that – Per-Ser-Vilient. I am perservilient. Okay, stay with me now, as this word will be in the dictionary one day.

Perservilient means I don't see stop, or am deeply unstoppable. Now, it is inevitable; stop will come knocking at your door. Usually, when we get a knock at the door, we will ask, "What?" or "Who is it?" or take a look through the peephole or out of the window, but this time you just open the door and BAM, you are greeted with a shocking, gut-wrenching punch that knocks you to your knees. Now let's be clear, everyone's stop is different and very personal, and what knocks you to your knees may not knock another to theirs, and that is okay; no one else's tragedy, devastation, or pain lessens yours.

Understanding the three phases of perservilience is essential. First, you must crawl, then you can walk, and finally, you are ready to F.L.Y.

Crawl: I remember the day *stop* came knocking at my door, and I forgot to ask, "What? Who is it?" I just opened the door and was struck by a gut-wrenching punch that knocked me down. I had just gotten home from work; it was the first day of a new job. I had a bad toothache and felt like I had dirt in one eye. I remember walking past my bathroom mirror and was horrified to see that one side of my face drooped. It seemed like my chin was on my chest, and one eye looked huge. I turned to my ten-year-old daughter and asked if something was wrong with my face. She replied, "No, Mommy." Years later, she told me that if I couldn't see that my face had fallen, she wasn't going to tell me. Kids.

I soon learned it was Bell's palsy, which is fairly common and can be caused by a virus. You probably know someone that has had it; you may have it, or you will know someone that will have it. There is no confirmed etiology or cause; it can just happen. Bell's palsy causes facial paralysis and can look like you are having a stroke. A high majority of people that get it recover within six months, but a small percentage of people, like me, don't quite recover their ability to move their face.

Imagine walking past the mirror and not recognizing yourself. I felt like a freak. I had plans to dance for the world, but after facial paralysis, I did not want my face to be seen, especially on camera. I stopped taking pictures, didn't allow videos, and cell phone cameras weren't welcome. I was incapable of smiling the way I did before, so I refused to do anything publicly because of how crooked my face appeared, and to this day, I still feel the same. The worst is when someone tells me to smile for a picture; that one comment instantly brings tears to my eyes. You might think something like a broken neck would take me out, but Bell's palsy was more damaging to my well-being and mindset.

I am telling my story to say this – you can't stop! *This* is where you start to become perservilient.

Imagine driving through a horrible storm, and the passenger in your car keeps telling you to pull over. You see all of the other vehicles on the road pulling over, but you've made up your mind and decided not to stop, even if you are moving at a crawl. You must get where you need to be and keep going until you are through the storm. You turn to your passenger and ask what happened to the people that stopped. They are still working their way through the storm. We must allow ourselves to feel the shock, depression, pain, and sorrow so we can move to the next phase of being perservilient – stand up and walk.

Stand up and Walk: This is a place of acceptance and beginning to figure out how to get back into *life*. It's the starting place for turning devastation into something positive. If you recall, I could no longer dance, had closed my school, and was living with a half-frozen face. At this point, I knew I needed to create a new twist to my dreams. Enter Ms. Ro's Dance Closet – my dancewear boutique.

Ms. Ro's Dance Closet allowed me to remain in the dance world by staying connected with and mentoring young dancers in my community. As a matter of fact, one of my former students, Ashley Rose, assisted me in my store. She was one of the first dance students at my school, had been a part of my life since she was eight, and I felt like she was my child. We called each other mother-in-love and daughter-in-love (a play on in-laws). We also had a rare medical condition in common; I had Bell's palsy, and she had Erb's palsy.

Erb's palsy is a paralysis of the arm caused by injury to the upper arm's main nerves, specifically the severing of the upper trunk. These injuries arise most commonly, but not exclusively, during a difficult birth. Ashley Roses' collarbone was broken during birth, and nerves were damaged. After she graduated from college, we decided to create a foundation geared toward empowering young girls and women with rare conditions, i.e., Bell's palsy, Erb's palsy, Vitiligo, Albinism, Alopecia, Keloids, Eczema, and so many more. We wanted to be living examples of strength, inspiration, and being perservilient.

So I was really in my comfort zone. I was not just walking; I was running in my second phase of being perservilient. This was perfect for me because now she was the face of the business. She was a young, beautiful, people person who loved the camera and spotlight. In contrast, I preferred all the behind-the-scenes business stuff. And then, knock, knock, knock, I forgot to ask, "What? Who is it?"

On June 15th, 2016, I got a phone call that no parent ever wants to receive. Ashley had been tragically killed in a car accident. Beyond losing my business partner, I lost my daughter-in-love of more than eighteen years. I don't even know when I fell to my knees, I just saw white. I was beyond devastated. I loved her so much.

Listen, people! *Stop* is going to keep knocking on your door, and you must walk through every emotion, truly feel and process it, and then accept it in order to get to phase three – F.L.Y.

Time to F.L.Y.: You must become who you want to be to F.L.Y. I lost one of the true loves of my life, but if I let our mission die with her, then I would not be honoring her, myself, or the people we vowed to help. That's what life is about, lifting others up. It was time for me to become the best example of my own advice, as I am known for saying, "You are beautiful, you are strong, and you can do anything!" Yet, I would just be a hypocrite if I weren't believing it or doing it for myself.

One night I was asked to be the keynote speaker at a women's empowerment event, and they wanted me to share my story. On this night, I decided this was how I could fully embrace and complete phase three of being perservilient, and I gave myself permission to F.L.Y. With the help of my audience, I decided to do a Facebook live and show my smile to the world for the first time – just put it out there for everyone to see. With all my smile's crookedness, looking like I was missing front teeth and all, I was about to go live, and I told the audience to get their lipstick on because I was only doing this once. Live in 5...4...3...2...1.

"Hey Facebook, this is your girl Roshawn or Ms. Ro., coming to you live from the I Am Awards, where we are honoring fabulous entrepreneurial women." As I panned the audience, I continued, "So, for those of you who don't know, I have a condition called Bell's palsy. It is a condition that causes partial paralysis of the face, and my face is paralyzed on one side. That's the reason you never see me smile in pictures. Tonight I will share my smile with you because I am going to be the face of a foundation I created called Permission To F.L.Y., and today, with these lovely sisters and queens supporting me, I have given myself permission to F.L.Y.-fully love yourself. So, cheese! There it is! You will see me on Facebook live a lot more to inspire and advocate. We also created a new word tonight called perservilient, which means we don't see stop; we are unstoppable. Gotta go! Say good night, everybody!"

I felt so liberated after the live. I was proud of myself. My teenage daughter was there to support me but was also watching me conquer fear and thrive. She came up to me sobbing uncontrollably. I didn't understand and was concerned for her. I asked her what was wrong, and she said, "I am so, so proud of you. You are perservilient." My heart was beyond full.

The Permission To F.L.Y. organization gives out a Persevilient award every year to a woman that has made it through her storm with style, dignity, and grace. We want you to know that Permission To F.L.Y. is not giving you permission but telling you, *you have always had* permission to fully love yourself because you are unstoppable. *You* are perservilient.

ABOUT THE AUTHOR

Roshawn Dorsey is the proud owner of Ms. Ro's Dance Closet, a dancewear boutique located in the heart of Historic College Park, GA. Her lifelong passion for dance and her desire to support her community of dancers of all skin tones drives her to stay active in her community. She was appointed to the College Park Main Street Board of Directors and is a member of the College Park Cultural Arts Council and The City of South Fulton Arts Commission.

In 2009, the stress of running a dance studio and healing from two major car accidents caused facial paralysis from Bell's palsy. This led to her co-founding a non-profit organization, Permission to F.L.Y. (Fully Love Yourself), in 2015. Permission to F.L.Y. empowers and inspires girls and women with rare/visible medical conditions, such as Bell's palsy, Vitiligo, Erb's palsy, Discoid Lupus, and Albinism, to push for their dreams. She hopes that telling her story will inspire more young women to fully love and embrace themselves no matter their story.

She is the proud mother of two daughters, Destiny and Bree, and grandmother to Cordé and Daija.

Connect with Roshawn at permissiontoflyinfo@gmail.com.

Connect with Roshawn:

 /permission_to_fly_/

 www.facebook.com/permissiontofli

🌐 www.permissiontofly.org

7

My Path to Self-Love

Tamara Wiedersum

Maintal, Germany

Who am I? What is my purpose, and how will my future look? Why do I look like this? Why me? These questions and more swirled around my head as a teenager while at school, looking in the mirror, or before going to sleep, and they would not let go of me. I was born with a paralyzed face, which will never go away. The doctors didn't know why it happened, and I often felt like my life was a big red question mark. There came a time in my life when I hated to look in a mirror only to see my unsymmetrical face staring back at me. Other kids teased me relentlessly, so the less I saw of myself, the better, and I would pretend everything was fine.

Although I didn't want to look at myself, I looked at other girls and envied them more than I should have because I did not consider myself beautiful. They all seemed perfect to me with their bright smiles. When I was with them, I always felt like the weird one; the different one. I always wished to be like them instead of like me. Anxiety was a daily state from the unkind and hurtful words blasted at me by people who didn't understand how their words affected me. One hot summer, I spent all my lunchtime hiding from the other students. I was teased and tormented endlessly about my paralyzed face, and I also didn't want to be bullied about my visible legs due to the shorts I was wearing. I had been traumatized by daily reminders that I was different and didn't fit in. So much so that I began to question everything about myself: my clothes, my weight, and even my height, which I could do no more about than my paralyzed face. When you are told every day you are ugly, you eventually begin to believe it. But not everyone was so horrific towards me.

Those closest to me were my strength and encouragement through my treacherous teenage years. My sister became my defender. Whenever her classmates spewed horrendous words about me, she would get mad and tell them how wrong and mean they were to say such things. She could handle it if her classmates teased her, but if they bullied me indirectly through her, it made her furious. She always lifted me up with her words and told me I was a great sister and that I was pretty and talented in music and dancing. In addition, I always had my parents and nice teachers who asked about my day or how I was doing. They didn't just say it because they felt bad but were genuinely interested.

Being self-conscious and sometimes feeling like a burden, I didn't want to make a fuss about the bullying. At that time, every day was the same. People were mean and would continue to be mean. I had to figure out how to stay surrounded by those who loved me and build my strength and confidence in that place of safety so that when I entered the world, I could handle the stares, ugly comments, and downright bullying. I would tell myself not to worry and that I was okay. I didn't know back then that because of the love and safety at home, I would get stronger. In time, I wouldn't care about the bullying, and eventually, it would stop.

But before the strength, I endured a lot. There were days when soccer balls were thrown at me on my way home from school, or my report card was purposely soaked in water. I could dwell on all the ugly, negative ways I was treated with a list as long as forever, but I prefer to tell you about three experiences that I am thankful for because they began to restore my faith in people and build my self-confidence and self-worth.

The first impactful incident happened during eighth grade when I was still insecure and thought nobody would react to the mean actions of my classmates. We used to switch places randomly in class from time to time, and I was always afraid to get seated near the mean kids. On one unlucky day, I was seated right next to the kid who bullied me the most. He annoyed me every single day until he did something absolutely crazy and was caught by the teacher. Our classroom was small, and the seats butted up against the windows. We would frequently open and close them depending on the day. If you were sitting at a desk near the window, you would have to lay flat over your desk to move the window. On this day, he pretended to close a window and told me it was clear to sit up. I hit my head hard enough that the pain was striking. Fortunately, the teacher saw it and reacted immediately, banning him from the next school trip. The result was that I began to trust my teachers to advocate for me, as my mother had always done. I didn't feel alone, and I knew if they cared so much about me, I must be worthy, right?

Another day, some kids were pushing me with great strength into the cupboard. They literally took my breath away with the force they used. A fellow student, but not a friend, stood up for me by telling the others to STOP! The mean kids immediately let go of me, and I am still thankful for his help. Years after, I thanked him for saving me by standing with me and for having the courage to stop the cruel kids.

Finally, came the day when I proved to myself that I could stand up for myself. Most kids weren't really bullying me anymore, but one kid still tried. This time, he failed! The computer room door could only be opened from the inside. He thought it would be funny to keep me from going in and just sat there looking at me with a smirk on his face through the door window. My friends inside noticed and opened the door for me. Then they told him how childish he was acting. As I walked past him, he was still grinning at me madly, but I didn't let it get to me. I felt confident enough to pat his shoulder, look him straight in the eye, and sarcastically tell him that he "did well" right to his face. He never did that again, and on that day, I realized I didn't care about the mean words and actions of others anymore.

When I was younger, I read books during break time because I didn't fit in with the others. I was happy for the slightest support I was given, and I was that nerdy little kid who loved talking to teachers. I felt like adults understood and liked me. But as I got older and went through different experiences, I realized that I was indeed pretty and loveable the way I was. I made friends and discovered my love for music and dance, which strengthened me. It became a way to cope.

Whenever I felt bad, I would randomly dance around my room, imagining my own small world, feeling the music, and only concentrating on myself. When I was sad, I loved to sit down at my piano and allow my fingers to play what my heart felt. I sang songs while crying and wrote songs about how I was bullied. Once I even started writing a song during class because I felt beyond annoyed. Writing down everything that made me feel sad or annoyed helped me to feel better; it was like writing a diary to myself. Writing helped me to get all my problems and worries off my chest. Music and dance were – and still are – my outlet and remedy. It's how I got through those torturous years.

Slowly, I began to allow myself to acknowledge that I was artistic and good at music and dance. I began to realize that I was a good and whole person who had a space in the world just for me. Other people's opinions of me didn't matter. I also didn't want to hide anymore. I spent too many years of my life hiding from my surroundings, hiding my face so nobody could see it. I really wanted to stop that and show everyone who I was and what I could do. That's when I joined Instagram.

At first, I didn't show my entire face in pictures because I still was afraid that people on the internet would be mean to me, just like in my school days. I knew how mean people could be on the internet. However, I was wrong. After I posted my first full-face selfie, I received dozens of comments and private messages, cheering me up and telling me how awesome I was to share my story. That's when things began to change, and I started sharing my activities, thoughts, and moments of my life with facial palsy for anyone who cared to look. People's opinions of me still didn't matter, and I had the power to ignore nasty comments and appreciate the good and kind ones.

I have reached many people since making my presence known on Instagram. Followers worldwide have asked for help and seem to feel comforted when they see my smiling face and encouraging captions that show what I feel inside. Through my posts, they have found support and someone to hold hands with. I get to be the kind of person I would have wanted to find for myself back in high school when I felt alone because of my facial palsy. I felt like nobody could understand me, even if they tried. When others tried to comfort me, it was nice, but I longed for someone who could say those words to me that I am now sharing with my Instagram community. Now I have a community of great people on social media that relate to me and my feelings, which is amazing! We share our stories and relate to each other so well. Facial palsy can have many different causes, and each story has its own character. I love listening to every single one.

Our stories might have started sadly, and some of us still might have a long way to self-love ahead, but our smiles are our superpower, and we should never forget that!

ABOUT THE AUTHOR

Tamara Wiedersum holds her Bachelor's degree in Southeast Asian Studies and Korean Studies from the Goethe University in Frankfurt, Germany. Currently, she works as a marketing assistant for a Korean provincial organization. She has been a Korean enthusiast since she was sixteen years old.

She was born with facial paralysis, and doctors don't know its cause or reason. Even though the cause of her paralysis remains a mystery, she enjoys writing about and sharing the ups and downs of living with facial paralysis to spread awareness. Sharing her experiences has helped many young mothers who have babies with facial palsy, and her reason for writing her chapter stems from wanting to inspire and lift others.

Tamara lives with her boyfriend, Thomas, who makes her feel like the most beautiful woman in the world, and his dog, Luna, and cat, Akiko. She creatively expresses herself through dance, singing, and writing songs.

She is even known to go live on social media, sharing her life experiences.

Connect with Tamara on Instagram /norena_96.

Connect with Tamara:

 /tamara.wiedersum

 @norena3897

 /norena_96

8

Pour It Out

Heather Pate

Near San Antonio, TX, USA

It's taken me 21 years to get to the point where I can be real with myself and open up with my story. I'm doing this to encourage and help strengthen someone going through the same thing or something similar and finally heal the little 9-year-old girl inside me who learned to bottle up her emotions because nobody she knew could relate.

The day I came down with facial paralysis (FP), I was swimming in my aunt's neighborhood pool. While my eyes were closed, I didn't realize how close I was to the side of the pool and ended up smacking my face on the wall – typical clumsy me. I was fine, or so I thought until we all dried off and returned to my aunt's house. I walked into the living room from changing out of my swimsuit, and my oldest sister immediately asked me, "Why are you making that funny face?" I asked her, "What funny face?" And she told me to go look in the mirror. Little did I know that this first look would rock my world and shift my entire way of thinking. This first look was when social anxiety, insecurities, and self-doubt became my new norm.

I vaguely remember looking at my droopy left side when the FP struck, but I feel my brain has blocked out the first few months of living with it, which indicates how traumatic and stressful it was for my young brain to process. However, I'll never forget when I went to my first appointment with my doctor. I can't remember in which order the tests began, but I do know that the hospital staff performed an MRI, CT scan, electrotherapy, and a sleep study on me. All the tests were either unsuccessful or showed no signs of why my nerves were damaged. For some reason, I have this vivid memory of telling the doctor that I hit my face on the side of the pool, but he told me that slightly hitting it could not have caused the FP.

In 2001, there wasn't very much information on FP, especially in adolescents, so my parents were advised to help me with facial exercises and massages to help stimulate the nerves and that they would more than likely come back over time. I was relieved to know this. I remember that anytime I hopped into my dad's lap on the couch, he would always get me to work on facial expressions and try to regain the movement in the left side of my face. When I practiced mimicking his facial expressions, it always bothered me deep down because it reminded me that my face was crooked or different from my other three siblings. Although one of my favorite exercises he used to do with me was to create a "wind tunnel." He would pucker his lips and blow forceful air out that would meet my somewhat forceful air when I tried blowing out with my semi-puckered lips. It forced me to practice puckering, but it didn't seem like practice because it was SO MUCH FUN creating a tornado-like sound with our wind tunnels. I'll never forget how we got to giggling when we tried to see how long we could keep our wind tunnels going.

Boy, do I owe my siblings! They taught me to find the humor in my dysfunction. I can't remember how it all started, but I would always get a laugh out of them whenever I covered the right side of my face (the working side) with my hand so they couldn't tell when I was laughing, and my non-working side would show a blank stare. However, after a while, when I realized the harsh reality of my face never returning to its normal state, this ongoing joke began to bother me deep down. It made me feel like I was someone to be made fun of, a clown. As time passed, I subconsciously taught myself to restrict my facial expressions because I became so self-conscious about people noticing my face was different. When photographed, I preferred to be on the right side, and if I got caught on the left side, I either avoided the picture altogether or made a goofy face so that my FP seemed intentional.

I'm very blessed that my mother took on homeschooling my three siblings and me because I didn't have to worry about being made fun of regularly; I just needed to worry about my own thoughts and feelings. Since no one I personally knew had dealt with FP, I taught myself to bottle my emotions. This practice caused me to internalize almost every issue I encountered, and I put up walls to prevent other people from getting to know the real me – the hurt me. I became a people pleaser because I felt it was the only way people would like me, and I rarely stood up for myself. I was unhappy with my appearance, so I became hyper-critical of my actions and words, preventing me from whole-heartedly pursuing many of my passions in life, like singing.

Around 11-12 years old, I began to worry about my future and whether I would find a husband. I remember praying for him regularly after I spent time crying and begging God to make the FP go away. Specifically, I would pray for my future husband's heart and that he would be able to lead me well because I knew it was going to take a special man to marry me. This was the age I discovered I was pretty (like my parents had been saying all along), even with my crooked smile, so I started dating. I had the opportunity to date some solid guys over the years, but if they were too nice or had a lot going for them, it would intimidate me, and I didn't feel worthy of being in that relationship. If it isn't obvious by now, I usually went for the bad guys or less-intimidating guys.

This dating decision was another destructive path for me. And after dealing with the loss of my brother in 2004, then moving to Florida at 15 after growing up in Louisiana, everything seemed to spiral out of control. I loved the idea of moving to Florida and had a blast the first year, but trying to make friends proved difficult. I'm not proud of many of the choices I made. However, it always felt like God was in the midst of all of those silly choices, ensuring my safety. He definitely provided a way out when He brought my future husband into the picture. I knew I had to get my act together if I wanted to pursue any relationship with him because he was the opposite of what I usually went for in a guy; he was extremely handsome, nice, charming, and ambitious. And almost instantly, I did straighten up. We started dating in 2010, and we have been inseparable ever since. God exceeded my own expectations of what my husband would look like and be like, and this was truly one of my deepest desires in life. My husband is my confidant, encourager, and best friend. He's taken the time to understand who I am and how he can support me on my healing journey, and I'm forever grateful for the man God designed him to be.

While getting married and starting our life together has been nothing short of amazing, in the past couple of years, struggles have brought a lot of unhealed childhood wounds to the surface for me. At the end of 2021, I began searching and reading other people's stories about living with FP after realizing that I still struggle physically and mentally with the aftereffects (synkinesis). While searching, I discovered Barbie Wharton's Instagram page (@BellsPalsyTalk), and she's helped me gain the courage to be more open about my story on social media. I started making other friends who have gone through the same thing, and it's been so refreshing speaking with people who can relate, even if they are online. After developing these connections, I picked my search back up to find ways to heal, and I've learned so much about what I really think caused my FP and how I can improve my thought patterns regarding myself and my appearance.

Three significant things have helped me improve my mood and well-being. First, I studied what our nervous system does to survive traumatic experiences. Understanding the four different trauma responses (fight, flight, freeze, and fawn) and which one(s) I acquired over the course of having FP guided my healing and flourishing. A gratitude journal is the second major thing I've used to improve my thought patterns. In 2021, I began using one to write about things that I needed to acknowledge in my efforts to move forward. Finally, I've focused on my physical and mental health through exercise. Exercising is a fantastic stress reliever and creates confidence in our bodies. In 2020, my family and I began transitioning out of the military and moved from New Mexico to Texas. I wasn't consistent with my workouts during this time and noticed that my stress levels were higher than usual. Once things settled after our move, my husband and I decided to join a local cross-training gym, and we noticed that our stress levels reduced significantly in a short period of time.

Being open with my story has been one of the scariest decisions I've made, but it's also been extremely rewarding. I feel like I'm finally being honest with myself and discovering who I was and who I ultimately want to be. At any stage in your facial paralysis, I encourage you to open the metaphorical bottle that contains all your fears, hurts, and frustrations and pour it out! Whether it's by writing or sharing with someone you trust who won't squash or minimize your feelings – Pour. It. Out. Regularly visit the bottle to ensure you're not holding on to things unintentionally because you'll go through periods of feeling great and then wonder what's happening when you start feeling weighed down. Give yourself grace in your healing journey, invest in yourself, and know that you are stronger than you realize.

ABOUT THE AUTHOR

Heather Pate is a stay-at-home mom, content creator, and health & wellness enthusiast. In 2017, she realized that her mission was to encourage women in their health & wellness endeavors. She continues to share with her followers that it's possible to prioritize health while being a busy mama - without feeling guilty.

In 2001, at nine years old, Heather endured a minor face injury while swimming in a pool and believes that heavy metals in her white blood cells played a role in blocking communication between her facial nerves and the seventh cranial nerve. Heather's traumatic experience with the resulting paralysis is why she shares her story and aspires to help others process their trauma and maximize their potential.

Opening up about her life experiences has helped her accept herself, while being a wife, mother, and CrossFitter have helped her gain confidence in most areas of her life. She believes setbacks can be moments of refining with the right outlook. You can find Heather playing her guitar and singing when she gets a moment to herself.

Connect with Heather on Instagram /Heather_Pate3.

Connect with Heather:

[instagram] /Heather_Pate3

9

Selfish Self Care

Andrea DiGiovanni

New Jersey, USA

M y story began one day in 2009 when I woke up and realized someone had shut the sound off, and I couldn't hear anything. I wrote it off as something obscure, like a wax buildup or the start of an ear infection, and sought an ENT. I found out I had something called a Cholesteatoma in both ears, which sounds daunting, but I didn't think so at the time.

Cholesteatoma: *"A cholesteatoma is an abnormal, noncancerous growth that forms behind the eardrum or from the eardrum. It's like a cyst that contains skin cells and connective tissue. Without treatment, the mass continues growing. Some cholesteatomas become large. In rare cases, they cause permanent hearing loss and other serious complications."*[1] It can even cause death.

It didn't sound like something horrible (well, maybe the death part, but I didn't know about that at first); it just sounded like I needed to get my ears cleaned. Unfortunately, for me, it was more than that.

Once diagnosed, I was informed the doctor I was seeing no longer performed surgery. He did have recommendations for a doctor in New York City, but I decided to stay close to home and chose a local doctor.

Thirteen years later, I have had time to reflect on my choices. I wish I had been diligent and had taken the time to find doctors who knew about this condition and had experience with the surgery. I had never heard of my disease before, and despite having access to the internet, I didn't know how to find the "best" doctor. Looking back, I wish I had spent more time researching and had listened to my original doctor's recommendation. This was a serious issue that I didn't appreciate, and if I had thought of myself instead of all my obligations, I most likely wouldn't be writing for this book about losing my smile due to facial paralysis.

When I allow myself to think about it, I find I berate myself for not doing a better job of finding a more qualified doctor. I should have taken my health more seriously, not just rushed into it on a wing and a prayer hoping for the best. I had two small children and didn't want to be away from them. I also had a full-time job and believed the downtime would be minimal. I honestly didn't know what I was in for and didn't think I would lose so much of myself in the process. I didn't know I wouldn't be able to smile again.

Who thinks about losing the ability to smile? Doctors always brush off the "what-ifs" of surgery, so I followed their lead and did the same. The doctor was so confident, and when she brushed over facial paralysis, I even smiled because I was so relieved I had found someone who could fix my issue. To this day, I will never forget that moment in her office as I was scheduled for surgery. I didn't consider that smiling was so much a part of me, and I took it for granted. It's like the ability to wake up each morning and get out of bed to do your everyday mundane, ordinary life activities. I just knew my smile would always be there.

It was like a permanent piece of body armor that I could rely on when I needed defense and protection. I could flash a smile to get out of trouble, get something I wanted, and keep dangerous threats at bay. I could also use it to flatter and disarm others. We've all heard the saying, "Smile, and the whole world smiles with you." I took this to heart and truly loved to smile, and if I am so vain to admit it, smiling looked beautiful on me. Without my smile, I didn't know who I was. I was not a quitter; however, if I didn't have children that needed me, I don't know but that I would have succumbed to the darkness that swallowed me when I lost my smile.

Let me touch on the dark days because those define who I am currently. I woke up from surgery feeling disconnected and knowing something was wrong. The doctor wrote it off as temporary, but for me, I felt so completely broken. Here I was with a jigsaw amount of stitches behind my ear, an orchestra of bells sounding off in my head, and this stiff face with an eye that wouldn't close. I rested as much as I could. I had to pull myself together for my family and work. At the time, I worked directly with the public, and there was no way to hide my facial paralysis. It was hard to speak, and my eye wouldn't close.

I HATED myself. I would go home from work and cry. I started avoiding mirrors and stopped making plans with friends. As my ears healed, I continued to regress. I felt like a monster. I wanted to go to sleep and never wake up from this nightmare. I did think about ending my life, but God had other plans for me. My youngest son needed me since he was diagnosed with Autism. I believe that truly saved me. I focused on him instead of myself. When the darkest days finally cleared, I was able to rise from the ashes. I decided this would not define me. I am here for a reason, and I know that now.

My advice to anyone who can relate to my journey is to do your due diligence when looking for your medical team and take the time to heal properly, both physically and emotionally. Self-love is of the utmost importance. Look into every doctor and treatment option available, and get as many opinions as possible to feel confident in the results. Look into the "what-ifs." Get advice and seek peer groups that might pertain to whatever is happening with you. I took the "easy route," and it ended up not being paved the way I would've liked. I was trying to be unselfish by ensuring I was ever-present for my children and continuing to work at my pre-condition pace. For these reasons, I went with the first local doctor I found and ended up with sub-par medical care and results that lengthened my pain and healing process.

By attempting NOT to be selfish, I erased myself from my own life. I became a shell of myself because I lost the ability to feel pretty and lovable. I was so damaged that I didn't think I could rise from the ashes. However, I have prevailed. I have moved on from this nightmare. I have found my voice and a way to be ok with where I am in my healing journey. I even found a way to smile again. It might not be the smile I mourn, but it's something.

Remember this "*Self-care is not selfish. You cannot serve from an empty vessel.*" ~ *Eleanor Brown*. Let that sink in. It is okay to feel bad for yourself.

It is okay to take the harder path to get the desired results. This is your life, and it's important to care for and be kind to yourself. Although I was attempting to heal and repair damage, I wish I had realized that instead of making me whole again, all the surgeries I would have after 2009 would take parts of my life away that I would never get back.

Through all this, I have learned a lot about myself and what I can withstand. I have discovered the way I can give back and help others is to use my voice to guide those who come behind me and encourage them that as difficult as it feels to be selfish at the moment, it is one of the most unselfish things they can do for their family and loved ones. Because with the proper care, they can heal and be whole again much quicker than if they choose quick and easy, but not necessarily what's best.

---

1. Cholesteatoma: Symptoms & Treatment (clevelandclinic.org). https://my.clevelandclinic.org/health/treatments/21535-cholesteatoma

ABOUT THE AUTHOR

Andrea DiGiovanni is a wife and mother of two teenagers and two rescued dog princesses (pit mixes). For over 25 years, she has worked in local government, but when she isn't working to conquer the world of purchasing, she is at home reading or just relaxing with her family.

Life took a turn for Andrea in 2009 when facial paralysis became her norm after complications from ear surgery, aka cholesteatoma surgery. She has tried not to let it get to her and is motivated to spread as much kindness as possible. She decided to share her story to further her recovery from the trauma of her experience and also to help others know that it's okay to feel whatever they feel and that no one can diminish your light. Andrea hopes to inspire people not to give up and to continue to smile their smiles, just like her.

Andrea can be found with her feet planted on the Jersey Shore.

10

Brave Face

Michael Ammons

San Diego, CA, USA

It was the summer of 2015, after ten years of living with facial paralysis and just existing in life. Two close friends invited me to attend a local community event called "Landmark." I was hesitant to go for many reasons, but primarily because of my bilateral facial paralysis due to Bell's palsy. I went to this event wondering how to explain this medical condition to a hundred complete strangers. I remember speaking as if nothing was wrong with me. All the while, my heart was racing, and my brain was running out of control with worry. I had to tell my brain to stop, or I would have walked out of the event.

As the event progressed, the audience was asked to get into groups of six to eight people. I immediately felt nervous because now I was being asked to get into a smaller intimate group of strangers. I remember sitting in the circle thinking, "What am I going to share?" and "How do I speak without my Bell's palsy being obvious?" and "How can I make facial expressions that don't look weird?" It was my turn to speak, and instantly I had this out-of-body experience. When I opened my mouth to share my facial paralysis, I told everyone how I had been living with the idea that my addiction had caused this lifetime condition called Bell's palsy.

Looking back, I remember fumbling with my fingers and being nervous. It showed as I started to speak faster, and my words began to slur. I had to calm myself by taking a deep breath and forcing myself to slow down. To my surprise, a group member spoke up when I finished speaking and said, "I have had Bell's palsy, too!" I was excited to meet someone who knew exactly what I was experiencing. I felt connected to him, and we formed a bond many wouldn't understand.

This event was intended to introduce some courses that would be transformative. When I signed up for the first course, I didn't know what was about to happen or that it would change my life forever. All the while, the voices in my head kept telling me, "You can't do this; you have Bell's palsy," or, "I'm too afraid to expose myself." What I really wanted was for my feelings of sadness, anxiety, confusion, anger, and desperation to go away.

I attended the first training course the next month. I remember sitting in a room with over 130 strangers, observing and thinking I couldn't do this. My heart started racing, and my face started twitching as it always did when I felt anxious. I sat in my chair and just listened to others' stories. Every time I wanted to raise my hand bravely, I talked myself out of it. I feared walking to the front to speak to the entire room of strangers while trying to hide my bilateral Bell's palsy and thought it might be more than I could handle.

After many attempts, I mustered the courage to volunteer and went up on the stage. I wanted to share a story that would make the audience laugh. But my brain had a mind of its own. At times it shouted, "They know something is wrong with you; you are only fooling yourself." Other times, my brain said, "They don't understand you. They look puzzled by how your face isn't moving much." It was so mentally exhausting trying to be funny, share my story, and hide my Bell's palsy simultaneously.

I shared about a time in college when we were doing team exercises, and I was asked, "Who was the first President of the United States?" My response was, "Abraham Lincoln." I was so embarrassed as everyone gasped and laughed. I immediately corrected myself by saying that I knew it was George Washington. It was a great laugh. Getting on that stage to share an embarrassing moment foreshadowed my journey toward peace and acceptance within myself.

As the course continued, my insecurities kept me from participating in the remainder of the program. I remember telling myself, "Ok, you did it once – now they know. Now what?" I would just sit there in my seat, battling my inner voice, which was screaming at me all the negative things, such as "You're broken, you're a recovering addict, and no one will love you for who you are." I experienced a lot of negative self-talk, which was emotionally draining. I wanted a different life than what I was living. I had to figure out a way to accept myself.

Even with all the negativity in my mind, I didn't let it stop me from my commitment. I pushed forward and signed up for the second course. I could see the possibilities. In the application process, I had to write down a breakthrough I wanted to experience in this next course. I immediately shared about living with Bell's palsy since 2005, wanting to be free of the crippling negative self-talk, and accepting what I couldn't control. The leader gave me an exercise that changed my life. She had me close my eyes and be present with my facial paralysis and all the emotions I'd ever felt. I began crying and just wanted it to go away. It was too much to bear. The grief was pouring out of me in an unstoppable manner. The leader simply said, "Let go of everything you're feeling in your face."

As I write this, the goosebumps are flooding back. It was like her words gave me permission I never knew I needed, and I immediately felt like the world had been lifted off my shoulders. I felt at peace for the first time. I couldn't stop crying from the freedom I was experiencing. I was free of anxiety, sadness, loneliness, and anger for the first time in over ten years. So, I continued to register for courses over the next several years.

In 2016, I took a leadership course and wanted to be a team leader. Doing this was out of my comfort zone and scary. I had spent most of my life telling myself that I would not amount to anything and that people wouldn't accept me for who I was. At different times, I thought ending my life would be easier. I always felt I had to prove I was worthy of love. It was time to confront my innermost thoughts – those horrifying thoughts that never in a million years would I have ever spoken to another person. Those thoughts of disgust and being less than others. I felt overwhelmed. I defined myself as a recovering addict with Bell's palsy who wasn't worth anyone's time. How dare I attempt to be a team leader for a worldwide leadership program?

Becoming a team leader would challenge me to the core of my being, and I would have to confront my inner demons. My training was about becoming an effective leader, and I knew this was the breakthrough I wanted for my life. Every quarter, a thousand participants would gather to attend this global leadership training program in different cities within the United States. We would go before the entire audience during the training to deliver a speech.

While waiting in line, my heart was beating so fast that I felt it would jump out of my chest. My body was shaking, and my hands were sweating as I walked on stage in front of the large audience waiting to hear my words. I was extremely nervous, but I reminded myself no one knew I had Bell's palsy. The first speech was a bust. One of the global leaders said, "You need to do that again and lighten up." I laughed and said, "Ok!" I took off my suit jacket and wiggled my body to loosen up. They played high-energy dance music, which allowed me to get into my groove and relax enough to do some dance moves. At that moment, I felt free to be me and released all the anxiety and nervousness. My second attempt was successful. I walked off stage feeling accomplished.

That experience left me empowered like I could take on the world. I now knew that my Bell's palsy was secondary to what I could accomplish. My negative emotions disappeared at this time. I felt free to share about living with Bell's palsy when I spoke too fast and slurred my words, and people couldn't understand me. I was liberated. I started living my life freely and choosing who, where, and when to share my story about Bell's palsy. I started going out socially with family and friends again. I didn't stay home and hide behind a dating app. I no longer needed to hide from the world.

Choosing to face my fears (pun intended), I found someone with whom I could have conversations, and we shared what we were looking for in life. I shared about my Bell's palsy experience, its impact on my life, and how my journey got me to this point. We dated for two years. On July

13, 2019, I proposed to him at Disneyland in front of the castle. We were married in June 2020. We have created a beautiful life together. He loves me for everything I am, my Bell's palsy included.

For almost 15 years of my life, I allowed Bell's palsy to keep me from living my life. I didn't know how I was going to get through each day. I've experienced every emotion that a person can have, and it wasn't until I took a chance on myself and enrolled in those courses that I transformed my life. Now, I live my best life. Getting Bell's palsy wasn't a choice. However, I choose how to deal with this condition on a short-term and long-term basis. It was worth the ten-year emotional rollercoaster to get a place of freedom while living with Bell's palsy. I hope my story helps one person have the same opportunity to live freely with Bell's palsy.

ABOUT THE AUTHOR

Michael Ammons is married to his husband, Ramon. He has a Bachelor's degree in Organizational Leadership and works as a nonclinical medical professional for a Southern California Hospital. He is a Union MAT Leader with AFSCME that represents 27,000+ University of California workers. Since 2016, he has helped to transform lives as an Empowerment Mentor.

A mini-stroke in April 2005 left him with bilateral facial paralysis. Michael decided to write for this book as a way to spread hope and empower others to live free by removing barriers and taking recovery one day at a time. He is living proof that people can manifest their path in life while helping others.

Hungry for the outdoor sun, Michael loves summers at the beach, soaking up the sun, and can be found at the gym lifting weights. He enjoys nature hikes and energizing six-mile walks on the boardwalk. He doesn't miss an opportunity to visit Disneyland monthly or to sneak off for a weekend trip to Las Vegas!

Connect with Michael on his website at www.braveface1.com

Connect with Michael:

/bravefaceguy

https://www.facebook.com/michael.ammons.33

11

Accepting My Reflection

Kristiene Harp

St. Petersburg, FL, USA

O n August 1st, 2020, I experienced one of my life's most transformative moments. At the height of the COVID-19 pandemic, I was thirty-six weeks pregnant with my first child. Panic and disbelief took over as I attempted countless times to raise my eyebrows and smile – to no avail. My reaction went from laughter to tears very quickly as I made the self-diagnosis of Bell's palsy. The condition was something that I was familiar with because my mother had it as a young teenager. She never fully recovered, and I was keenly aware of what it had done to her confidence.

Crazily enough, I still went grocery shopping even after getting advice from a nurse to go to the Emergency Department. After shopping, my husband and I finally went to the hospital, where they prescribed steroids. I saw improvements almost immediately, and in just one week, my face recovered significantly. I thought my worries were over when I took my last dose of the prescription on August 10th. That was also the day my son was born – the best day of my life!

Eight days later, I observed that I was starting to look like myself again. I mentioned this to my husband, who agreed, and I felt I would soon be as good as new. That night, after waking up to nurse my newborn, I went to wash my hands in the bathroom. Glancing in the mirror, I saw a nightmare. My face was yet again paralyzed, but this time the paralysis was on the opposite side. No, it can't be. I convinced myself I was overly tired and went to bed, *praying* that my mind was fooling me.

The next morning, I placed one hand on either side of my face while smiling to brace myself before the mirror confirmed my biggest fear. I immediately noticed full function on my right side and complete immobility on my left. After looking in the mirror, I couldn't control the tears. Thankfully, my parents had flown into town as my postpartum supporters. Lord knows I needed them.

To say I crumbled in my mama's arms is an understatement, but I was soothed by the prayer my daddy said over me. The physical and emotional burden I felt that day was so heavy. I was recovering from labor and dealing with engorgement from breastfeeding with an unrecognizable face. With so much pain, I felt like my body was no longer in my control, and I had an intense fear of never recovering or another episode reoccurring.

I returned to the Emergency Department for treatment, but they denied me, as they were prioritizing COVID patients. I felt defeated. Days later, I *finally* got in contact with my primary care provider, who prescribed another round of steroids, but it may have been too late to be effective. I didn't know how things would turn out, but I prayed that the steroids would cure me.

My parents left a few days later, and I instantly felt regretful. I hadn't taken full advantage of their help, and my husband had only a week of paternity leave remaining. I would be left to figure things out on my own, which was daunting. My new-mom anxiety was at an all-time high, and I feared being unable to juggle motherhood and the struggles that seemed to be increasing with my condition.

Unfortunately, the second episode of Bell's palsy was far worse than the first. A week after onset, I experienced incredible pains behind my ear, and my tastebuds were painfully swollen on the left side of my tongue. I had no sense of taste, and tinnitus haunted me daily. For the next three months, I woke up touching my cheeks, hoping for movement, to no avail.

An MRI showed no evidence of other causes for my paralysis, and my neurologist said it would just be a waiting game. At this point, I was feeling like a medical freak. No one could tell me the cause, why I had the rare occurrence of it happening to me twice, or why these occurrences happened so closely together. I sought physical therapy, where I regained a decent amount of movement. However, my physical therapist wasn't listening to my concerns about a side effect that I was developing (synkinesis). He had never heard of it and told me it would probably go away on its own and that full recovery wasn't realistic six months after the onset. As the six-month mark neared, I started feeling hopeless and stopped treatments.

It was tough. Looking back, I put way too much pressure on myself during that time. My primary focus was to be a good mother and a great wife. My husband never pressured me, yet I prioritized having him come home to a clean house and a nice dinner instead of getting much-needed rest. I did this because I wanted things to remain how they had always been despite the changes in our family dynamic.

Caring for my newborn son was unbearable at times. I wish I had taken the advice to sleep when the baby sleeps because I paid for it in extreme exhaustion. As a result of the palsy, sounds became amplified, and the baby's cries caused stabbing pains in my highly sensitive ear. Along with exhaustion, loneliness was also an all-encompassing feeling. Our little family lived in an uneventful military town, away from the people who loved us. If only we had been home, I just *know* that time of my life would have looked entirely different. I say this because I am currently with my family as my husband is deployed, and I'm receiving excellent support – something I wish I'd had back then.

It's been two years now, and I'm making a conscious effort to grow my confidence. I've never had the highest self-esteem, and as a teen, I'd constantly nitpick my appearance. However, in the months leading up to my Bell's palsy, I was close to fully accepting myself. Now, I sometimes feel as if I have gone back to my teenage years – except I'm not comparing myself to anyone else, just the image I *used* to see in the mirror. Pictures are hard and social settings are sometimes awkward with new *and* familiar people. I'm very cautious about smiling "too hard" as it exposes my lack of facial symmetry.

I still have a lot of anxiety and fear surrounding my Bell's palsy. When I notice any symptoms I experienced at onset (i.e., a severe migraine, tinnitus, etc.), I'm afraid I may wake up to a paralyzed face again. After joining a Facebook group for people living with facial paralysis, I'm aware of others who have also had it multiple times. Because of this, I worry about my next pregnancy, as pregnant women are more likely to develop Bell's palsy than the general population. Despite my concerns, I refuse to allow the possibility of recurrence to stop me from growing my family.

Regretfully, I allowed my mind to be in a state of negativity and hopelessness for over a year. As a result, I hardly have any pictures with my son in his first year of life. Not being able to express my joy in this new chapter of motherhood was exceptionally difficult, yet I wish I had soaked it up more. I am now putting in the effort to relax and enjoy the toddler stage with my son. He keeps me going, and I owe it to him to be more present.

On a positive note, I've acquired numerous invaluable gains that I could never trade for the loss of my smile. To name a few, I gave birth to a beautiful, *healthy* baby boy and developed an even stronger bond with my husband, who was my rock throughout my frequent meltdowns. I also grew in my understanding of what self-care truly means, and my faith in God increased as I had to rely on Him to get me through these difficult times.

This experience made me realize how little I cared *for* and *about* myself. I often ignored my body when tired, hungry, or emotionally drained. I was also a "yes man," especially in my military career. Even when I was going through terrible pains during my pregnancy, I suffered in silence, never mentioning it to my leadership. At the same time, I had a right-sided tooth infection that I couldn't get treatment for until after my son was born. With the stress of the pandemic, work, pregnancy, and the infected tooth, I often wonder if this perfect storm may have caused my Bell's palsy.

Even after acquiring Bell's palsy, I neglected my body. Until now, I hadn't given it enough credit for the incredible work it did. Despite skipping meals, I produced ample amounts of milk for my son for 19 months while the nation experienced recalls and shortages in baby formula. I made a full recovery from my labor wounds within the expected timeframe. Although I did not fully recover from my paralysis, I am able to function almost normally in tasks that were once difficult, like eating and speaking. The healing in my body was truly miraculous.

I've also learned to be more assertive about getting the medical attention I need. I understand the issues that medical facilities faced during the pandemic. However, I could have gotten treated at another hospital instead of going without care for days when I had my second episode. And I could have requested a new physical therapist soon after I realized I wasn't being heard. This experience has made me aware of the need to be my own advocate, and I appreciate that I can apply this knowledge in the future.

One thing that I would like any reader to know is that it's okay to be upset about things that happen unexpectedly. I used to guilt-trip myself because I was agonizing over a condition that wasn't life-threatening. As my therapist explained, having Bell's palsy meant substantial personal loss, and losses require a grieving period. Grieving time is different for everyone, but no matter how long it takes, it is fine, and all feelings are valid during the process.

Having never taken my smile for granted, I had been told there was a warmth about me because of how friendly and welcoming it was. It has taken a while, but I realize now that despite the circumstances, I can still radiate that same energy with my new slanted grin. The kind person I've always been still remains inside.

Ultimately, my desire is to no longer be on a hunt for my smile but on a lifelong journey of self-love. I am starting this journey by accepting what I cannot control and changing the things I can. It's time to start living! I may never get my smile back, but I *can* exercise, eat healthier, find my best angles in pictures, and get the rest I need. I can also dress with more care, as my wardrobe (consisting of black oversized frumpy clothing) has reflected my inner struggles. With these changes, I hope to finally not see a damaged version of myself in the mirror. I just want to see me, Krissy.

While writing my story has aided me in moving forward in a positive direction, my goal is to let others know and feel that they are *not* alone. I'm grateful to you as a reader and hope to have inspired you to love yourself!

ABOUT THE AUTHOR

Kristiene Harp, also known as Krissy, is a wife, veteran, and stay-at-home mom. She graduated from St. Petersburg College with her Bachelor's degree in Interdisciplinary Studies (Summa Cum Laude). A year after marrying her sweetheart, Krissy and her husband enlisted in the US Army, where she was awarded an ARCOM for her stellar work ethic.

In August 2020, during her first pregnancy, Krissy experienced the first of two episodes of Bell's palsy and had very rare bilateral facial paralysis. As writing her chapter has acted as the springboard to her own journey of self-acceptance and inner healing, Krissy hopes to inspire others to cultivate a deep love for themselves. While The Hunt for My Smile collaborative is Krissy's first published literature, she is thoroughly considering the idea of writing a book of her own.

Krissy's passions are her family, food, and music. In her spare time, you may find Krissy creating handmade necklaces and bracelets from old and broken jewelry.

Connect with Krissy at krissystakeaway@gmail.com.

Connect with Krissy:

/krissystakeaway

@krissystakeaway

www.krissystakeaway.com

12

Special

Mary Freed

Calgary, Canada

M y symptoms started on a Friday night in early July 2022. I had an earache, and it hurt to touch the side of my head. Simple, I thought, I must be getting an ear infection. The following day, while eating my beloved Shawarma, I noticed I hardly had any taste and couldn't feel the inside of my mouth on the left side. I concluded I must have Covid, but my test was negative. When I woke up Sunday morning, the left side of my face was completely paralyzed. My left eyelid was hanging low, blocking my vision. My cheek and lip were sagging like I had aged 20 years overnight. My eyebrow wouldn't budge, and my eye couldn't blink. Can you imagine sneezing and your eye staying wide open? The pain in my ear was so crazy and crippling that any sudden noise forced me to shrink and cover my ear. That's the day I discovered that my dogs bark a lot.

I saw my doctor on Monday, who wrote a letter so I could quickly get through the emergency room. Although he was very confident it was Bell's palsy, he had to rule out that it wasn't a stroke. That was the first time I feared my symptoms. As I drove to the hospital, I was thinking about my sons and ailing mother, who had just moved to a nursing home. I have been a widowed, single mother since my boys were toddlers. My mom's health had been declining for months, and she was struggling to adjust to living in assisted care. I was her only surviving family member. Who would look after her and my sons if something happened to me? I had been the lone caregiver for so many years, and it scared me to think I couldn't be there for them. Thankfully, the fantastic and supportive staff saw me quickly and confirmed it was Bell's palsy.

After leaving the hospital, I was on the phone STAT! I called my sports massage therapist, my acupuncturist, and a physiotherapist. Everything my doctor told me to do, I did. I booked everything I could immediately because I wanted to heal as fast as possible.

I was starting a new job the next day and decided to message my new boss to let her know what was happening. She offered to allow me to begin a week later, but I knew enough to realize that the facial paralysis wasn't going away anytime soon. I declined the offer and showed up for my first day. It's hard to explain how embarrassing and awkward the first day was. My hearing was impacted, and it felt like I was hearing underwater. I had to resist the sudden urge to cry because I didn't feel like myself and wanted to hide my face entirely. I had only been paralyzed for two days and was still trying to figure out how to eat and drink, not to mention talk. I somehow survived my first week. I noticed there were a lot of staring eyes but also a lot of kindness. Then, I faced another hit when my mom passed away the following week.

My mom's passing was very sudden but not surprising. I was in complete shock and was in survival mode with my face. I had so many treatments booked that it took me a few days to cry for my mom. Then I realized I could only cry on one side of my face. I was so angry – I couldn't even cry properly. I felt so low and isolated at that moment. I often think about how the last time my mom saw me, my face was crooked. I didn't want that to be my mom's last memory of how I looked. I knew she was worried but unable to understand what had happened to me. How could she? I didn't understand either. I wish I had reassured her I would do everything possible to get better, but time ran out.

The first few weeks were especially hard for me because I couldn't – nor did I want to do any of my normal activities. I am hugely active; I box, run, cycle, and weight train, and I have two coaches and a fantastic fitness community. I was so ashamed and embarrassed by how I looked I just couldn't go to my gyms. I was open about my diagnosis on social media, but that was easy for me. Being in person is another story. I tried going for a bike ride, which was impossible; the wind was too harsh on my non-blinking eye. We had beautiful summer weather, and I couldn't enjoy riding my motorcycle because of my vision. For nearly two weeks, I went to work at my new job with my best foot forward and my bubbly personality, and then crumbled when I got home. Both of my sons were at a loss for words. I have an amazing, supportive family, but it didn't matter what anyone said; I was stuck in my own negative thoughts.

Then a couple of weeks later, I said, "Enough!" I missed all my sports and my community. I had to face this and be brave. I realized I didn't know how long this would be with me, and I hated how negative I felt, so off I went. I booked training sessions with my coaches, and my regular schedule resumed. It was not easy facing people at the gyms. There were a lot of questions – the worst question by far was, "What happened to your face?" People didn't know how to ask. I found myself answering questions with confidence and knowledge because people need to know about this; it could happen to anyone. The best question I received from one of my gym buddies, who still asks me every time he sees me, was, "How is your health?" I can't explain the kindness I felt in this question.

Between my fitness schedule and all my "face appointments," as I liked to call them, I started feeling like myself. I noticed that I didn't wake up and run to the mirror immediately to look for overnight improvements. I also discovered my new obsession, straws. I have straws everywhere now, and it's a bad day when I leave home without my straw. Straws have taken over for what used to be numerous chapsticks everywhere. I have mastered eating Pho soup without making a huge mess on myself, but I would never have that soup in public.

The best day came when I decided I would give my cycling bike another try. I was not feeling optimistic, but I missed cycling so much. I geared up and put on my cycling glasses. After about a block, I was riding away with my big half-face smile, and my eye was ok – what a fantastic feeling! I felt so grateful. When I arrived home, as I was putting my bike in the garage, I found myself saying out loud to no one, "I don't even care what I look like; I just want to do all my stuff." This was a big moment for me, and I think about it often. I was just thankful I had come so far physically that I could return to my routine.

Along with massage, physiotherapy, and acupuncture, it was also suggested I try Float Tank therapy. This therapy was a game changer, and I highly recommend it to anyone who needs more quiet moments to themselves. Floating in a tank of salt water with no pressure on the muscles or limbs and having a still mind is amazing for the body and mental health. I recently started treatment with a naturopath who altered my diet and implemented small amounts of Chinese Medicine that have helped my health overall. My diagnosis has led me to focus more on self-care and setting boundaries when situations or people are causing me distress. I'm learning to take a step back and take care of myself first.

My uncle has called me "special" for a long time. I don't think I am special, but I believe this journey with Bell's palsy and the healing process afterward was meant to happen for a reason. When the opportunity to write about my experience arose, I was eager to share and help, but I didn't realize the healing I would receive from being a part of a collaborative group of authors who all have facial paralysis. I now know I am not alone and that these special people totally understand what I am going through. I know I have a long road ahead of me, and I don't know what my entire recovery will look like, but I'm not giving up. I want to support others and their healing path. I am a friend and a listener, and I will loan you a straw if you need one.

-Mary

ABOUT THE AUTHOR

Mary Freed has had a successful career in the Oil & Gas industry for many years and enjoys her job as a Risk Analyst.

In July 2022, Bell's palsy struck and caused facial paralysis. Mary decided to share her story to bring hope to those who suffer from the condition. She wants to spread the message that it does get better and that it's part of the healing journey to have awesome days and bad days. The opportunity to talk about her experience, offer hope, and inspire others is part of her recovery process.

Along with a huge extended family, she has three sons and three grandchildren. She also has a lot of love for her pets, which include three dogs, a cat, and a snake. In her spare time, you will find her with a pair of boxing gloves on, weight training, cycling, running, or out with her dogs. Mary was a late bloomer discovering her passion for fitness and has not looked back. She is always striving to be "younger next year."

Connect with Mary at maryfreed03@gmail.com.

Connect with Mary:

/usmegos/

/3megos

13

Coffee Date with RHS and Cancer

Ferial Abdoel

Den Haag, the Netherlands

I was at Haga Hospital, the largest hospital in The Hague in the Netherlands, on a gloomy Wednesday afternoon in February 2022. While there, a surgeon informed me there was a malignant lump in my left breast. At the same time, she noticed the drooping of my mouth and my unblinking right eye.

I wasn't surprised that I had cancer; I had not been feeling well since the end of 2021. I had been feeling drained and tired, but my face not reacting was strange. I hadn't noticed it at that time as my painful ear and cramped neck were a bigger concern.

At first, the doctors thought I was having a stroke because of the facial paralysis, and after being tested, Bell's palsy was mentioned. I also had a severe sodium deficiency, so instead of returning home and processing the fact that I had breast cancer, I ended up at the neurology ward with a drip in my arm and compromised balance.

The days after my admittance to the hospital, I endured two MRI scans (head and breast) and epidural injections. While in the hospital, I was utterly confused and unable to pronounce my words properly. I had difficulty eating, lost control of my face and balance, and was unable to blink. All of this was in addition to dealing with the fact I had cancer. It was like ending up in an episode of the Twilight Zone, a real-life horror story.

After two days, I saw an ENT who diagnosed me with Ramsay Hunt syndrome (RHS), as I had the telltale signs of blistering in and around my ear. Another classic symptom was that I could not close my eye; therefore, I learned to tape my eye shut in the evening and at night, so I could sleep. RHS is Shingles (caused by the herpes zoster oticus virus) that affects the facial nerve near one ear. I was prescribed antivirals and Prednisolone.

Fortunately, after five days at Haga Hospital, I returned home to my husband, Dirk, and my cat, Ziggy, and slept in my own bed. I attempted the daunting process of understanding what happened to me and tried to figure out how to deal with having both RHS *and* breast cancer. The initial relief of being at home disappeared as the virus hit me so severely that I couldn't eat, sleep, walk, or be my active, boisterous self. I became lethargic and had never felt so miserable before.

I contacted my nutritionist as I was losing a significant amount of weight (7 kg within three weeks): RHS was taking all my energy, and I had all but forgotten about the cancer.

I was placed on liquid nutrition to help me regain some strength; I could hardly sit up straight, let alone stand or walk independently. I had to be pushed around in a wheelchair by Dirk, and then I was eventually able to start using a stroller for my first walks outside the house.

I was determined to walk by myself in March and beat both RHS and cancer. I tried to find as much information on RHS as possible, which was scarce compared to the available information on cancer, as it didn't seem to be an issue in the Netherlands.

My mum & Dirk accompanied me initially during my first short walks, and then I went on my own for longer stretches to build stamina and get well enough for the cancer treatment. I was fed up with being at home, unable to work, go out for a film or dinner, travel, or enjoy life as I used to.

I started taking photos and used them as a kind of image diary. The cherry blossoms had started to bloom and were a great inspiration for my lens, with their delicate pale pink petals, like tiny blushing faces smiling at me.

I had already decided I would not do chemotherapy; I was still too weak, but I also wanted to get rid of the tumor. By this time, I had nicknamed it "the parasite" as it was an unwanted presence bleeding my body of energy.

After speaking with my oncologist, we decided I would have surgery in April, followed by radiation therapy. I shall never forget how I walked into the operating room with my eye taped shut and using the IV drip holder to keep my balance. I am thankful for the outstanding surgeons who did a glorious job pulling me through this ordeal and encouraging me to have faith.

Hours of desperation alternated with hours of determination. I never stopped seeing the beauty of the people and the world around me, and

I never stopped taking photos. While recovering on the twelfth floor, I took shots of the high rise of the city center, The Hague, and the glorious sunsets. I even wrote a haiku after my first operation, wanting to capture the moment and feel alive.

I recovered through April and May from surgery and radiotherapy and worked to regain my balance so I could go for longer walks. I also started reading books again, made simple meals, and felt more like myself.

I found I had more time and energy for contemplation. As I look back, those first months were a period of great confusion and loss for me, losing my health and facial movement. I went from being a happy, healthy, active person to being a dependent, depressed person who was stuck at home. This change was extremely difficult to deal with, not to mention the fact that I had to stop working and lost my job.

Like so many others worldwide, I endured a lot of stress during COVID with the fear of getting severely ill, the endless lockdowns, and the isolation. Stress is a major cause of illness and death, and I was trying to endure too much stress at work. Aware of this, I returned to meditation, breathing exercises, and eating more fruit and vegetables. I focused on being mindful and grateful. By the end of April, I was ready for walks on my own and started with a visit to the library, where I found I could finally read again.

This library was one of the first public places I went to, and being welcomed by the library staff was heartwarming; I almost cried. Previously, I had been a regular visitor, often going every week or two, so returning there after two months felt both wonderful and strange.

In the following weeks, I started to visit more often, not only for books but also to read magazines, and after not drinking coffee for months, I sipped cappuccinos or flat whites, and this brought back some joy again. I also enjoyed watching people as they talked and leafed through books.

The reading room was like an extension of my living room. After being stuck at home for such a long time, with limited visitors, it was the first opportunity to socialize with people other than my circle of family, friends, and hospital staff since my devastating diagnosis.

My face was still paralyzed, and I was anxious about interacting in public. Thankfully, the people at the library showed kindness and care toward me as they had known me for years. It was daunting to go out by myself, and I was apprehensive about how people would react to my paralyzed face. Fortunately, despite my flaccid face and losing my big toothy smile, I did not receive any weird or rude reactions.

Eventually, I broadened my daily walks and went further from home. The Hague is the only big city near the coast of the North Sea, with two beach resorts, and Scheveningen is the one frequented by tourists. Kijkduin is lesser known and just a twenty-minute walk from my apartment. So, I would hop on the bus with my books, walk down to the dunes to one of the beach clubs, sit outside on a nice cushioned bench, and order a delicious cup of coffee.

This was the first fresh brewed coffee I had tasted in months (the coffee in the library being automat coffee), so I took my time to savor the smell and taste of it. I sat facing the sea with the brilliant sun shining on my face, attempting to keep a smile that matched my huge inner grin. Grateful is how I would describe the feeling of once again sitting near the sea, listening to the sound of the waves, watching the gulls play and laugh (I was sharing a bit of my syrupy cookie with them), and feeling the wind on my mostly fallen face. Just shy of feeling happy again, I was certainly glad to be alive.

I ordered another coffee in the company of Ramsay Hunt syndrome and breast cancer and told them that they wouldn't stop me from going outside, reading books, going to libraries and cinemas, having dinner, or enjoying life. I told them I would walk home, continue to recover and do the things I'd always enjoyed, like art, literature, music, nature, travel, helping animals and people, and life in general. I had lost so much, but I was slowly getting back my abilities and, most importantly, myself.

Many cups of coffee (and tea) followed, but the memory of that first cup of coffee at Kijkduin beach after being so severely ill will stay with me for the rest of my life. Next year, I will return to the same place, with my smile and laughter as I always used to; hopefully, I will be cancer-free.

Dear Reader, this journey of facial paralysis and breast cancer has taught me three things.

First, be kind to yourself, especially when nothing seems to work out, you're feeling miserable, or you're unable to do anything. If possible, try to enjoy the things you love doing. In my case, I started to go for walks, read again, and meet up with friends. Be your own best friend.

Second, be patient with yourself, the illness, and the healing process. At times the process of healing is even more difficult than being ill. I follow the example of snails, who go about in their slow, quiet, yet very strong ways. It is easier said than done, but it does help.

Third, try to be in the present moment as much as possible. Being present allows for mindfulness, peace of mind, and quietness. Especially when I was sad, angry, or in pain, I used this to settle myself and relax.

I hope that if you find yourself dealing with multiple medical crises, you will remember these things, and they will help make your journey a bit easier. Thank you for reading my story.

ABOUT THE AUTHOR

Ferial Abdoel was born in Paramaribo, Surinam (a former Dutch colony in South America) and has lived in The Hague, city of peace and justice, in the Netherlands since 1969. She studied Japanese language and culture at the University of Leiden and worked for the Ministry of Foreign Affairs, Agriculture, and Justice and Peace, as well as the police force. Currently, she is focusing on writing professionally.

Ferial's facial paralysis, Ramsay Hunt syndrome, was triggered while fighting cancer in February 2022. Although she searched, information on healing and recovery was sparse in the Netherlands, which led her to contribute to this book. She hopes that people living with facial paralysis, and the medical professionals who treat them, will read this book and receive answers and hope for those beginning their recovery from facial paralysis.

Ferial and her husband, Dirk, enjoy long walks on the beach of Kijkduin, seafood dinners, and love their cat, Ziggy. She has returned to traveling and can be found reading, watching films, and going to gigs.

Connect with Ferial at ferial.abdoel@planet.nl.

Connect with Ferial:

   /poppy_ferial/

14

Strong

Renee Ramirez

Levelland, TX, USA

S trong, fierce, determined, pretty, bright eyes, beautiful, perfect smile. These words have described me most of my life, and I once held them as a standard of my worth and ability. If I did not fit what I believed these words meant, I needed to change my mindset or perception of the situation. All of that changed when I realized I would be living with bilateral Bell's palsy for an undetermined and potentially neverending time frame.

I had been told that complete recovery would take six weeks, and something dreadful happened in my heart when the six-week mark came and went. As a woman of faith who truly depended on God, the reality was that despite my continual praying, begging, boldly showing up at the Throne of Jesus, and asking for complete restoration and healing, it was not happening. Despite my family and friends interceding on my behalf, trusting God to heal me, speaking healing over my life, and putting all their faith and trust in God to heal me, it was not happening.

As the days passed, I realized something I had felt in my heart from the beginning; this would be my battle for longer than I would be able to handle in my own strength. I was upset and angry because I would no longer look the same, despite doctors promising that "it would all be gone in six weeks." I was promised I would wake up one day, and it would be gone as quickly as it came. I was told the unlimited rounds of prednisone were safe and effective. Repeatedly I was told that I had to wait at least six weeks, and if I had not healed by then, we would need to wait three months because "nearly everyone" heals within three months. Three months passed, and I was informed that I had waited too long for surgery that could have helped if it had been done between two and three months of diagnosis.

I was angry because I had done nothing to deserve this horrible curse that was negatively impacting my life. I was a graduate student pursuing a master's degree and was thrilled about my career prospects when I was struck with this life-changing facial paralysis. How would I present my thesis in front of two hundred graduate school students? How would I interview for jobs? Who would want to hire someone with drooping eyes, a face that struggles to smile, an eye that is noticeably smaller than the other, slurred speech, and unexplainable brain fog? Who would want to take a chance on a minority woman with facial paralysis?

I no longer felt strong, ambitious, fierce, or like a fighter. I felt helpless, weak, lost, and unheard. I was so used to praying and the outcome honestly coming out in my favor that I was utterly lost when it did not happen. I prided myself on the fact that I rarely asked others for help.

I would push through whatever challenge came at me, but now I didn't know how to fight this battle. I didn't know how to ask my loved ones to be the rocks I needed, to step in with the medical side of things, or to help me seek help. I didn't know how to ask everyone to stop telling me it would get better and that it was not noticeable. "Yes, people, it IS noticeable; please quit trying to pacify my emotions."

I didn't know how to explain that I had not lost hope or trust in God; instead, I realized that His plan was not healing. I also did not know how to accept or adjust to this reality. I found myself experiencing anger and frustration I had not experienced before. I had seen miracles in other people's lives and my own life. How could I live with the reality that this may be the path and the "thorn," as Paul would say, that I must carry in my life? I wish I had the answer to this question, and I wish there were an easy "accept it" button, but unfortunately, that is not the case.

I found myself in a state of depression. While on the outside, I remained happy, saying all the right things, continuing to thrive at work, and pushing through school, I was broken inside. I was no longer all those words people once used to describe me. I would look in the mirror, and the pretty, perfect smile was gone; the bright eyes were slowly looking sadder and even lost at times. I completely stopped wearing makeup and doing my hair; buns became the easy fix. And forget caring about my clothes; I was happy to wear scrubs to work. Moreover, having unlimited rounds of steroids contributed to massive weight gain, and I was up forty-plus pounds. The more I gained weight, the deeper the depression set in.

About six months into my diagnosis, I was forced to look at myself, deep dive, and ask, "Reneé, if this is the cross God has given you to bear, if this is to bring others to Him, if this is a part of your testimony to build His Kingdom, are you willing to accept it? Are you willing to let go of your anger at God? Are you willing to turn to Him in the grief and despair and trust Him, EVEN when you do not see Him answering your prayers? Will you continue to lean into Him, trust Him, obey Him, and allow Him to lead you? Reneé, are you willing to use your Bell's palsy story, or will you stay in your grief? Will you allow anger and bitterness to take over your life? Even though there is no reason to feel ashamed, will you allow yourself to feel shame? Will you bury yourself in sorrow until you completely lose who you are?"

These were difficult questions and a bit gut-wrenching for me to answer. While I had never given up on God, I was very angry and felt like this was some form of punishment that I could not possibly understand; the God I believed in did not punish His children in these ways.

Anyone with facial paralysis understands the frustration of trying to figure out the cause, which can be a rabbit hole we fall into, sometimes becoming a weight holding us down and keeping us from moving forward. I researched every medication I had taken, changes in household products, going to sleep with wet hair, going outside with wet hair, going outside without covering my ears when it was cold, using Q-tips; you name it, I researched it, desperately attempting to find out what the cause was. What had I done to cause this? I was full of guilt, so sure that somehow I had brought this upon myself.

I cried uncontrollably over the next few days, and it wasn't until weeks later that I realized I needed help. I threw myself spiritually, emotionally, and physically down at the foot of Jesus and said, "Ok, I am all in." I can't change or control what has happened, but I can control how I let it affect my life. I had trusted God with every aspect of my life when I was a missionary, and as I pursued my education, career choices, and relationship choices – it was time to trust God with this, as well.

I began researching other treatments for Bell's palsy. I realized small-town medicine was insufficient, and I had too many questions. I joined Facebook groups to hear others share their stories and found hope in things like acupuncture. I began to find my strength again. My graduate program pushed me to take a leave of absence to focus on healing as this was going to be the most challenging year, with my thesis being the primary focus. I refused. I would not allow myself to stop what I was doing because of Bell's palsy. I had not fought so hard to get where I was to let this thing take me down.

I started telling my family and friends what I was feeling, how I appreciated them, and that I was grateful they were not giving up hope that I would have complete healing. But I needed them to understand that I had to learn how to LIVE WITH Bell's palsy and explained that I needed them to support me right where I was. This meant not "correcting me" when I talked about living with facial paralysis but accepting that I needed to live in the space I was in currently.

I realized I did not know how to live with the acceptance of who I was with Bell's palsy, so I reached out for more help. I found an online therapist who understood when I said I wasn't comfortable with people seeing my face and never forced me to turn on my camera, instead letting me move at my own pace. I did more research and found a doctor in Chicago who was a facial paralysis specialist. I found the New York Facial Paralysis Center and scheduled a telemedicine appointment with Dr. O.

I powered through. I dug deep to fight the depression. I did not have an easy turnaround; it was by no means quick.

The appointment in Chicago left me with a relapse and ongoing pain. Dr. O. was excellent but did not feel there was anything she or her center could do. I still cried every night, felt weak, and didn't like what I saw in the mirror. I still felt lost at times, but I didn't stay there.

I opened my Bible and reminded myself what the Word of God said:

- Jeremiah 29:11-12 "For I know the plans I have for you, says the Lord, they are plans for good and not for disaster, to give you a hope and a future. In those days when you pray, I will listen."

"When you pray, I will listen." Those words became my lifeline. My prayers changed. I began praying that God would teach me and show me who I was and that He would show me how this facial paralysis had been used for good and how He could use it in the future. When I look back on my season of depression, I realize it was a grieving period. I was grieving who Reneé Ramirez once was. She was not bad; she was actually a pretty amazing woman. Reneé Ramirez pre–Bell's palsy had served her purpose; she had achieved and reached all she was supposed to, and now it was time for Reneé Ramirez with Bell's palsy to take over.

Daring, Determined, Inspiring, Roomy, Fighter, Honest, Inspirational, Spiritually Strong, Overcomer, Faithful, Amazing, Beautiful, and Persevering. These are the words people now use to describe me. They are engulfing who Reneé Ramirez, MJ is. Yup, MJ, I completed my Master of Jurisprudence in the midst of Bell's palsy. I applied for jobs I was not qualified for and dominated those interviews. I learned to hold my head high and not cower away from people or opportunities. I am a little in love with this new Reneé Ramirez.

ABOUT THE AUTHOR

Reneé Ramirez earned her BA in Criminal Justice from Angelo State University. In 2021, she received her Master of Jurisprudence in Compliance and Enterprise Risk Management from Loyola University Chicago. She served as a missionary in seventeen countries across the continents, including South America, Asia, Europe, and Africa.

In 2021, Bell's palsy caused bi-lateral facial paralysis for Reneé. She believes faith is the key to overcoming, surviving, and thriving through any obstacle and hopes this is the message readers will receive when reading her chapter. Her life motto has become, "lean into the hard things in life, the challenges that scare you, the obstacles that can break you, lean into them and watch what God can do."

Reneé often advocates for the "at-risk" and homeless communities, volunteers with Shared Hope International, and gives a voice to PCOS survivors. She comes from a close family with amazing parents and a sister who Reneé considers her inspiration. She is engaged to her junior high sweetheart, David, and enjoys being a bonus mom to their boys, Seth and Devyn.

Connect with Reneé at rramirez5105@gmail.com.

Connect with Reneé:

⊙ /pcos_princess_warrior/

f /renee.ramirez.lovesJesus

in /in/renee-ramirez-m-j-5322a41b7

♪ @bellspalsyprincess

15

Two-faced

Maria Rebecca Sias

Beaverton, OR, USA

It started with a simple earache. For two weeks, I dealt with the pain and agony, not knowing that soon my life would change forever. If I had known how wrong the doctors would be and what was to come that Sunday morning, November 21st, 2021, I might not have felt like my life had imploded. It turns out it wasn't an earache, and the doctors didn't know it was a symptom of something that turned out to be much worse.

I woke up that morning and knew right away something was noticeably different. The lips on the right side of my face were tingling with pins and needles, exactly like when my leg falls asleep. At first, I didn't think anything of it and did what I usually do when overwhelmed – I ignored it – until I looked in the mirror. I then realized that ignoring what was happening was not smart and possibly dangerous. The longer I looked at my reflection, the more my face seemed to fade away. In a worried haze, I blamed myself and went in search of my parents for comfort. When my dad locked eyes with me, he calmly said we needed to go to the hospital because something was very wrong.

At the hospital, the nurses took me back immediately, and after explaining the situation, they were helpful and kind and had me laughing, smiling, and feeling safe. Because of Covid procedures, my dad wasn't allowed to come in with me, so I was all alone. All I wanted was my dad. I was absolutely terrified, and I knew he would calm me. I took a deep breath, centered myself, locked down my terror, and waited to see the doctor. I met with the doctor, and after a brief exam, he diagnosed me with Bell's palsy, as I still had decent control and movement in my face. Being discharged from the ER and realizing that my visit only took an hour and a half when I thought I was having a stroke two hours before was scary and unnerving. I didn't know what to do or expect, although they told me that my body would need as much rest as possible (boy, was that an understatement). The doctor prescribed me the typical meds for this diagnosis and sent me home, but to be completely honest, I felt like the medication did nothing.

Unfortunately, the most devastating thing happened on the fourth day when I realized I had lost all movement on the right side of my face, including my smile. It was something I had taken for granted over the years. I had never let go of my smile, even though I had been through a lot. My smile was my favorite feature; I loved it. No matter what happened, it was always there and gave me the courage to fight. But, when I looked into the mirror that Wednesday morning... it was gone. My smile was gone, and this person staring back at me was not the person I had identified with for thirty-seven years. This person was a complete stranger. I had no idea what to do in this situation. What could I do? What was I supposed to do? Seek more help? How do you seek help when the doctors know little to nothing about this diagnosis, and the information they have is so inconsequential it's almost a myth? Anything I did find wasn't from the doctors but from other facial paralysis survivors.

Like a bad mantra or song, one question was continuously on repeat for weeks, "Why me, WHY ME?!?!" I had been going through a lot in my life and was trying to come to terms with those challenges. Why did this have to happen? I didn't understand at the time, but almost eleven months later, I understood better. As humans, we sometimes forget to slow down, rest, recharge and decompress. I had so much going on and wasn't listening to my body; it was screaming at me to slow down. The Universe intervened, "How in the world am I going to get this woman to slow the heck down??? BINGO, I got it!! I'll give her something she cannot ignore." Universe, I love ya, but you suck sometimes.

Those first four to five weeks were some of the worst I had ever experienced in my life. I was wading through extremely dark clouds, but through it all, I decided to focus on staying positive and finding the silver lining. I had to. The choices were either to remain optimistic or mentally spiral downward into the abyss. I had already spent years crawling out of that place and was unwilling to go there again. I refused to jeopardize my healing process by focusing on the wrong thing. It wasn't easy, and honestly, this was probably one of the most challenging situations I have had to overcome. There were days I just wanted to wallow in my sorrow and pain or sleep and never wake up, and when I did wake up, I hoped it had just been a horrible nightmare.

I began my search for a positive mindset, which would help me and my family cope with this situation and understand they could joke around with me about it. I didn't want them to hide or walk on eggshells around me. According to my youngest sister, Nina, she would crack up when I would laugh because half of my face wouldn't move, and she felt I resembled the Batman villain, Twoface. I don't think I have ever laughed so hard in my life. These small moments of joy gave me the strength to continue fighting for the day I would get my smile back.

I didn't have a plan for what positive things to focus on; I just took a deep breath and allowed things to flow naturally. I learned to trust the process and let some things go while appreciating others. The positivity I chose to live by soon became a close companion; when I needed her, she was there, and when I didn't, she patiently waited beneath the surface, ready to catch me if I fell.

I began to notice and had to adjust to new quirks. For example, relearning how to talk was an adventure, as I could no longer pronounce Bs and Ps. With my face paralyzed, I no longer had control of the muscles that make the B/P sound. When I would try, it was just a puff of air. Another thing I noticed was that I would make a low growling sound towards the end of the day when I was exhausted and couldn't concentrate enough to speak clearly. Think of Al Capon in The Godfather: "Say hello to my little friend." I could mimic it perfectly. There were suddenly a lot of quotes from movies or shows that I could mimic in style and tone, and this never failed to put a smile on my face and those around me. I could also mimic songs like "Bitches" by Mitchell Tenpenny with the newly acquired grittiness in my voice.

An entirely new world opened for me, and I began seeing things in a new light. It was like a lifesaving breath. I adore writing, whether poetry or short stories, and I focused on these new feelings, emotions, and thoughts as topics. I realized I had an overflowing and abundant pool of writing ideas from this experience. It's incredible how much my writing influenced my life for good this last year. Through my writing, I found I could release all the emotions – good and bad.

My kind heart is not broken,

She is tired.

My beautiful soul is not fragile,

She is fatigued.

My gentle spirit is not quivering,

She is exhausted.

Please do not mistake her peace and quiet for weakness, for if you flip the switch and disturb her peaceful rest, your burns will never heal, for her dark side is just as tired.

Writing was one of many things I found to stay optimistic about, and it saved my life. Positivity led me to believe I could keep going and gave me the strength to understand that I could find the good in everyday things. I found good in my sisters' smiles and laughter, my brothers' strength, my friends' support, my mother's guidance, and my father's love. A positive mindset helped me to deal with a condition that had no rhyme or reason, and I am proud of that.

I've learned all these months: positivity isn't about always being happy, joyful, or putting on a brave face to say that you're ok. It's understanding that you will also have bad days, even horrible days when you don't want to get out of bed, or mediocre days - neither bad nor good.

I fluctuated a lot in the early days. On one of my worsts days, no matter how much I tried to stay optimistic and work through each moment or how many coping mechanisms I used to stop the grief, they all failed me.

I cried and cried and cried, and finally, I chose to allow myself to feel. That day was a haze. I buried myself underneath the covers of my bed and raged in my sorrow as the tears began to flow into what seemed a tidal wave of never-ending heartbreak.

It was at this time that I came to realize I would never truly heal 100%. That was the hardest pill I have ever had to swallow. After some deep and hard conversations with my sisters and best

friend, I finally understood my life wasn't over. My journey was being rewritten with the ability to grow bigger than anything the Universe or I could have imagined.

When I first looked in the mirror, I saw a victim. Then I heard my own cries and screams and made a stand because I was reminded that I am a fighter. My family helped me find my way out of the dark. This is my story, and I want you to know that you are not alone. I see you, I hear you.

If you take only one thing from this, let it be that positivity isn't all-encompassing. It isn't constant, and you must understand that you will have bad days. There will be days that you struggle and don't feel like doing anything. Learn to embrace those days as well as the good. Find what positivity means to you, not what others say it is or how society defines it. What makes you feel optimistic, and what makes you feel joy and hope? When you turn your negatives into positives with endless possibilities, it's not about moving on but about moving forward and finding the good in the small things. Remember, life doesn't stop with this diagnosis, so why should you?

ABOUT THE AUTHOR

Maria Rebecca "Becky" Sias is a sister, daughter, partner, friend, and poet. Over fifteen years, she has gained skills as a jack-of-all-trades, having worked in the automotive industry and the Bon Appetit catering service kitchens at Intel. Currently, Becky works as a courier delivering books and supplies to the Washington County Cooperative Libraries.

In November 2021, Becky learned that Bell's palsy was the cause of her facial paralysis. When asked to share her story in this book, she was excited about the opportunity to help others. She plans to widen the scope in which she writes by sharing her poetry and short stories in her own book. Her first poetry book is in process, and she believes it will inspire the imaginations of children to trust they can do whatever they put their minds to.

Becky's favorite pastimes are spending time with her family and close friends and having random adventures with her favorite people. She's motivated by love and compassion, has a thirst for life, and has a passion for family.

Connect with Maria at favoritenumber2@gmail.com.

Connect with Maria:

 /fiestybex

 @afewsimpletters

16

What Palsy?

Anayansi Arias Iriarte

Panama City, Panama

This story is about the funny face my facial paralysis gave me; funny as in a funny "ha-ha" way and not as in a funny unbearable state of being...although I might add, Bell's palsy does make me feel just as overexposed as the closeup of the most famous funny face of all time: Audrey Hepburn. Her closeup, by Richard Avedon, inspired the movie remake of the musical *Funny Face*. For added effect, the song plays in a darkroom scene in which her famous features—her eyes, her eyebrows, and her mouth are the only things you see while Audrey and Fred Astaire float around to Gershwin's magical notes. Any similarity to living with Bell's palsy is pure coincidence!

The morning I discovered the mouthwash I was swishing around my mouth was spraying the mirror with rebellious spit in every direction, and my eyeball rivaled Alastor "Mad-Eye" Moody in Harry Potter's *Order of the Phoenix*, I burst out laughing. Yes, my go-to coping mechanism is laughter, which is what I've been doing since I was diagnosed with Bell's palsy on the right side of my face. I've been laughing it off as the most ridiculous joke life has played on me so far.

I was given both excellent and terrible advice those first few days after March 15, 2021, but the thing that worked wonders right away, and still does to this day, when I'm tired of doing what I've dubbed *facexercise*, is laughter. Nowadays, it is easy to find funny clips on your fave social media, from cats walking backward to babies being babies. And if you're not a fan of reality silliness, look up classics like *Monthy Python*, *The Three Stooges*, or my faves growing up in Panama, *La Tremenda Corte* with Trespatines or *El Chavo del Ocho* with Chespirito.

Laughing out loud relaxes my face to the point of not feeling it anymore, which is what most of us crooked bandits want. We dream of the day our lips and eyes stop twitching like Captain Hook's when he hears the "tic toc" sound announcing the imminent arrival of the crocodile approaching underneath his ship to swallow him whole. The only thing is, the palsy twitching needs no tic toc crocodile to set up shop on our faces. I chose to crack up laughing instead of ugly crying in desperation when I saw this happen in the mirror for the first time.

The word desperation does not even begin to cover the dreadful scenarios I dreamed up during the first five seconds of realizing that what was looking back at me in the mirror that Ides of March morning was not due to the lack of a proper prescription for contact lenses. I kneaded my cheekbones as if they were made of playdoh and moved my nose up and down and sideways for what felt like an entire day without much success in lifting my sagging face. The "Mad-Eye" Moody situation was another deal altogether. My brain just gave up on the closing eyelid maneuver after trying to shut the eyelid for hours. I became a hot mess, dissolved in tears, yelled till hoarse with a river of snot running down my neck, and all the while, a broken record of "what-am-I-gonna-do-now?" was playing in my ringing ears.

As a trained attorney, translator, and mediator, my face is one of the vital tools of the trade to convey the message I intend to deliver to my clients and the public. "HOW AM I GOING TO WORK WITH MY FACE LIKE THIS?!" The second those words were out of my mouth, I began to laugh maniacally. See, I had always complained of the stressful workload that just kept stacking up with no end in sight, and here it was, a gift from the prankster Universe: the best excuse to slow down and reorganize my life in accordance with my needs! I now had the perfect reason to work remotely!

However, it was far from easy. I sacrificed living with my boys, 7 and 14 years old at the time, and relocated to Panama, where I could get more affordable and personalized health care and therapy. The boys stayed in New Orleans with their father for nine months, and then by the end of the 2021-2022 school year, we agreed it would be best if the youngest came to live with me in Panama. We decided the oldest (now 16) would stay to finish high school under his father's supervision. Ironically, the facial paralysis stretched me as a mother, without the Elastigirl superpowers of bouncing back immediately!

I went from being a full-time parent on call 24/7 for my boys to being invisible to them for months so that I could focus on myself and my health. It took a lot of support and encouragement from my team of medical professionals to force me to see that if I didn't take the time to heal, I would never be able to return to the mom that I was. I turned to meditation and breathwork to help my mind get to a healthy place, and the benefits of this daily practice are still immeasurable in my healing process.

Meditation allowed me to recognize that the main cause of my facial paralysis was the pent-up stress accumulated over decades from using and abusing my mind and body. Bell's palsy is, in fact, a poisoned prize that I now choose to see as a never-ending gift. I meditate daily (my favorite practice is yoga Nidra) to discover a path to peace that may or may not help me recover my smile, but have no doubt, it helps me live my life. Isn't that what our real purpose is anyway? We all are where we are supposed to be. I have regained my "mom life" status and, with a few new tricks, continue improving my well-being.

In the end, life is but a moment, and what we are living right now as Bell's palsy survivors is a moment in time. Live, love, and most importantly, laugh – the harder, the better. Even the Mayo Clinic is on board with this advice: "A good laugh has great short-term effects. When you start to laugh, it doesn't just lighten your load mentally; it actually induces physical changes in your body."

Laughter can:

- Stimulate many organs. Laughter enhances your intake of oxygen-rich air, stimulates your heart, lungs, and muscles, and increases the endorphins released by your brain.

- Activate and relieve your stress response. A rollicking laugh fires up and then cools down your stress response, and it can increase and then decrease your heart rate and blood pressure. The result? A good, relaxed feeling.

- Soothe tension. Laughter can also stimulate circulation and aid muscle relaxation, which can help reduce some of the physical symptoms of stress.

What are you still doing here reading this hilarious essay about my funny face?! Go on now, kiss that beautiful face in the mirror, and brace yourself for the best laugh of your life; you just found out you're alive and kicking ass! And don't forget to breathe.

ABOUT THE AUTHOR

Anayansi Arias Iriarte is member 59,951 of the Cloud Appreciation Society as she loves to watch clouds while dreaming up stories and photographing anything and everything around her. She received her degree as a lawyer, mediator, and certified translator in English/Spanish/Italian in the early 1990s. Anayansi was born in Spain and has lived in Panamá, England, Costa Rica, and Italy. For the last 15 years, she has lived in New Orleans, LA, where she worked as a Museum Docent at the Ogden Museum of Southern Art while raising her two boys, now sixteen and nine.

She relocated back to Panamá in 2021 in an effort to recover from Bell's palsy (right-side facial paralysis), which she believes was a direct result of stress mismanagement. The absence of literature available for people with facial paralysis led her to share her story. Laughter is her primary coping mechanism, and she hopes to inspire others to laugh daily, even through trauma.

Anayansi laughs out loud daily thanks to Jacki and Amore, the two stray cats that rescued her, and Ale, the man she calls home.

Connect with Anayansi at traductoranayansi@gmail.com.

Connect with Anayansi:

[O] /paralisisdeque

17

Loving Myself in the In-Between

Cristina Toso

Vancouver, BC, Canada

T he last few years have been a journey of learning to love myself in between the times in my life that were easy for me to love. As I found strength at various stages of my journey, I have many stories of triumph, wisdom, and gratitude that could be inspiring, but my goal is to be real. It's in the authenticity where my strength exists, in the vulnerabilities of my life where I can learn, and in the challenges where I can listen, discover, and release to make room for something new. So maybe it's more meaningful to share the in-between and to know we're ok just where we are now, understanding that life isn't always a stage to display strength and triumph.

My journey began well before facial paralysis onset in 2018. I'd dealt with my fair share of serious chronic repercussions from sports injuries and other conditions. By far, the most life-altering of all resulted in major personality changes with the loss of non-verbal emotional expressions that had fully connected me to others before the paralysis. It took three months to regain any movement in half of my face. From there, I worked hard on my physical and emotional healing.

My new life contained a constant barrage of discomfort and torture with an eye that didn't blink properly and the unbearable cramping pain of synkinesis intertwined with the intense emotions of losing my original face long-term. By the end of each day, my facial muscles were so overworked that I felt like I was running the last bit of a long marathon where I had to push beyond the physical pain toward mental fortitude to get me to the finish line. However, *my* marathon was from normal day-to-day existence, such as eating, driving, talking, reading, walking, being awake, and even sleeping. You get it.

Two years in, I was a coach for a self-development program. While an essential part of my journey, coaching was hard on me during some of the workshop days. One of those workshops was a long, grueling fifteen-hour day, including drive time. What I remember the most about that day was not the battle with synkinesis. It wasn't the eye pain I endured that felt like a million tiny hot pins poking my eyeball. Grinding at my sanity was a combination of all those things coupled with the hyperacusis pain – the stabbing ear pain that had me feeling like someone was sticking a long, sharp pointy object into my brain through my ear canal and twisting it around. Every sound hurt because my brain was still not consistently innervating the stapedius muscle, the tiniest skeletal muscle in the body needed to temper sound, which is controlled by the facial nerve.

With the help of the head coaches, I found solutions to be fully present in a room with more than eighty people while enduring the leader's voice assaulting my ear via the sound system. I briefly left the seminar for relief, then bought earplugs and ibuprofen. Even though the pain was still there, eating away at my ability to stay sane, the earplugs helped. I wish I had thought about using them when first diagnosed.

These physical debilitations that screamed for me to rest quietly at home challenged my ability to express myself spontaneously and be freely present. I needed to keep it together for the participants I was coaching while also being authentic about my challenges. I desired to spontaneously smile as abundantly as I had always smiled prior to facial palsy, but I forced myself to suppress my emotions to minimize my facial movements. I wanted to be free, but it just wasn't possible.

This internal conflict escalated when interacting with my fellow coaches during an exercise. This exercise demanded exaggerated emotional expression, which meant I would feel physical pain, and they would see the degree of dysfunction I had attempted to minimize visually for two years. Having been an animated person before the palsy, holding my true emotional self back was like walking a tightrope with a carrot shoved up my ass while simultaneously being trapped inside a lifeless painting.

The emotional and physical challenges of the day led to a meltdown during our coach's post-workshop meeting when I volunteered to do an exercise with the leader. As I had a lot of grief, trauma, and anger locked up inside of me, the leader wanted to practice a technique with me to facilitate my freedom from it all. He had a tough time as the depth of my pain emerged more at every opportunity for a breakthrough, like the new skin of an onion emerging after peeling off the first layer.

Outside all this pain and utter exhaustion, many good things took place. I had supportive people around me wanting to find solutions so I could continue being present. The participants I was coaching saw value in me beyond my physical appearance. I worked on myself to push and re-discover purpose, satisfaction, and joy. Even though I was mortified that I burst my top like an overworked steam engine at the end of the day, I felt grateful. The people that surrounded me at that moment were trained to listen, be curious, and be present for something most had not experienced.

It wasn't until then that I realized how much I had bottled up since my facial paralysis diagnosis. Yet, until Covid-19 stress and mom's last journey with cancer later that year, I hadn't even begun to release the accumulating grief. I had been stubbornly working to shift my thoughts, live the way I wanted, and help others with facial palsy through support and education projects without allowing myself some space. I had wanted to be free from the physical debilitations weighing me down like an anchor sinking to the bottom of a lake instead of accepting my limitations and slowing down. Also, my passion for helping others with facial palsy took precedence over my own need for self-care, as it was more important for me to "conquer my situation" and contribute to others than it was to slow down.

Understanding how much I had pushed myself whenever I faced physical adversity rather than allowing myself to truly rest, release, and recalibrate, took two more years, even though I was aware of it for most of my life. I realized how much I had been living in the past, not the present. The cumulation of serious life events has persistently taught me that dreams sometimes burn up so new ones can emerge from the ashes like a rising phoenix. While discovering new dreams along my journey, I continued returning to old ones and expected my body to perform as it had when I first had those dreams.

Having waited so long to listen, I got to a place after mom died where I couldn't even do the simplest things without being out for the count for days recuperating. I had pushed my body beyond its limits to look after mom 24/7 at my parents' home over the last four days of her life, then remained awake, unable to rest shortly after. I had pushed through to the funeral, writing a eulogy and ensuring I could present mom to others with strength and positivity. No breaking down was possible for me at a time when her life needed to be honored.

New debilitating pain and dysfunction arose from that suppression. I got to a place where I lacked confidence in holding a part-time job out of fear that I would not be capable of reliably showing up due to all the physical things that would come up for me.

I had always worked diligently on myself and pushed through my body's limitations to lead a powerful life. And for a while, this worked. I was conquering my world and my limitations. I believed when breakdowns happened, I just had to keep pushing my way to achieve all I wanted despite the blocks that appeared.

I'm not so sure about that belief nearly five years post-onset. Some breakdowns are a desperate cry from my "body-mind" to listen. Listen to the exhaustion. Listen to the pain. Listen. Just listen. My body cannot do all I want it to do as it did before all the injuries and illnesses. Perhaps my mind is trying to light up some things that were suppressed in the only way it can – through the body.

As I write this, I have learned that there comes a time when it is essential to rest – actually rest. I had pretended to rest while still pushing my body and mind. Sure, pushing myself to live beyond limitations was important, but not at the expense of future wellness. My future wellness came in 2020, and I am now in a state of unwellness I have never felt before. I am climbing a mountain I created for myself, a massive mountain of tight turns, slippery slopes, treacherous drops, and daunting, insurmountable peaks and valleys that seem to take me in circles rather than up and over the mountain.

Why does this mountain seem insurmountable? Because I pushed too hard from the first serious injury at twenty-two to the moment I developed acute facial paralysis at forty-five. And I finally arrived at the point where I began losing my grip two years later. Instead of being the tortoise, I was the rabbit because I compared myself to non-injured folks pushing themselves beyond their limitations to achieve great things. However, I couldn't realistically run in the same race or even finish the race from which I didn't know I could simply step away.

Maybe I'll get this balance thing mastered one day. I know I will fly again. I always do. I now fully accept that my vessel requires greater maintenance and is limited in ways others' vessels aren't. I have an opportunity to adjust and maintain it in new ways and stop comparing myself to others. And when it comes to reaching mountain peaks, they will be different than the ones I had imagined I'd be on. That's okay. Letting go is not giving up.

The thing that facial paralysis has taught me more than anything else which I have endured is that resilience isn't about always having a smile on my face and being happy no matter what. I relied too heavily on this. It isn't about all the things I can continuously accomplish. I was stuck believing this for too long. It certainly is not a race to keep up with everyone else. No. Resilience is something more profound for me.

While I have tried all my life to listen to my body's communication, love it, and be grateful for it, I want to act on its behalf with greater integrity. Even if I feel my body fails me with increasing in-betweens, and I fail it in return, I can still choose to love it and love myself completely. This unconditional love is now the level of resilience I seek.

ABOUT THE AUTHOR

As a facial palsy advocate, Cristina Toso is passionate about creating awareness and building better access to authoritative knowledge. To assist others, she started a support group with a local therapist and worked with facial paralysis warriors to create an informational podcast episode. Cristina also collaborated with fellow author Ilan Livne on the Facial Paralysis Talks Informational Bot, built to help those newly experiencing facial paralysis find support. Soon, she plans to create a non-Facebook online community platform.

In March 2018, Cristina experienced facial palsy suspected to be Bell's palsy or Ramsay Hunt syndrome. Facial paralysis led her on a journey of re-discovering ways she could fully love herself and accept her body more. She hopes that her story will inspire others to tell their stories and to accept themselves no matter what.

Cristina is always looking for a doorway into nature, and she can be found kayaking, forest bathing, or gardening, depending on what her body allows.

Connect with Cristina at komorebitoso@gmail.com.

Connect with Cristina:

 /Facial Paralysis Talks

 Facial Paralysis Talks Podcast on iTunes

 Scan Here for access to the Facial Paralysis Talks Informational Bot

18

Bell's palsy: Before, During, After

Maryam El Amiri

Agadir, Morocco

My life story feels very typical to me, yet somehow special, too, because it impacted me in a way I could never have imagined. I grew up in a tiny city in Morocco, where nothing stressed me besides doing my daily homework and helping my mom with the household chores. I was always a calm and shy person around other people, and I never felt bad because I didn't have a social life; instead, I enjoyed being alone and in peace.

At 18, I went to the university for undergraduate studies and was shocked by how different I was from other students and how hard it was to adapt. Going to the university felt foreign, and I struggled to make friends because of my timid personality. In time, I made a few acquaintances and stayed busy with weekend plans or studying as a group. In my second year, I adapted well to the new environment, and sometimes, I traveled around exploring and learning about the area. I began to make new friends, but some of them turned out to be toxic and negatively impacted me.

Year by year, my studies increased in difficulty, especially during my junior year, so I was stressed a lot, even over simple things. As a result, I took a semester off because I was extremely overwhelmed by the difficulty level. I had minor depression, which took me a year to reconcile as I learned to adapt. Being at the university was overwhelming, and I had little positive social life. These things began to impact my health and well-being so severely that I couldn't handle them anymore, and that is when my story with Bell's palsy began.

On January 10th, the day of my university finals, I should've been able to breathe and relax after all the studying and focus on disconnecting from the online semester. Instead, I was diagnosed with Bell's palsy. At that time, I didn't think it was permanent, just something that would disappear in a few days. I was in denial, but it didn't just go away. That evening, I realized that I had no control over my face, and I asked my mother if she could do anything, but she didn't know what was happening, either. I tried to pull my face up, but without success, I felt terrible and lost, and I cried over and over, trying to wake up from the nightmare. For a moment, I regretted allowing myself to be stressed, but this was happening, and there was no going back, so I cried for hours!

The next day, I checked with a neurologist. He diagnosed me with Bell's palsy and asked me to do some physical therapy sessions. My mental state wasn't at its best, I was crying all the time, and I didn't like others staring at me. Looking in the mirror was scary, and taking pictures of my face made me feel down. However, my healing process would prove to be interesting once I discovered acupuncture; it was a magic treatment for me. Not only did it help to recover my face, but it also helped me to rest and improve my mental health, including my minor depression. It is almost impossible to explain, but it improved the state of my mind and body. I began to allow myself to recover and to rest, so acupuncture was a necessary process in my treatment, and I grew to appreciate that Bell's palsy gave me a chance to feel like myself again.

After the acupuncture treatment, I followed up with a home massage that my physiotherapist recommended. Overall, there was little improvement because it was hard for me to do it myself and to follow the guidelines as needed. The process for me was full of ups and down. I followed up with another physiotherapist that helped me to see improvement again, and I sometimes allowed myself time to cry during the sessions as I could not bear it anymore. I had no energy left. But the supportive people surrounding me were beneficial to my healing as I noticed small improvements in my face, which motivated me to keep going.

It's been one year and nine months of walking in my healing process. It's been slow, but my smile, which I've always loved, is returning. In reflection, it is hard to believe that I went through this whole experience because I didn't know how to manage stress. I believe that the physical and emotional parts of our bodies are connected to the point that our body actually expresses how we feel. My body expressed how it was feeling after years of stress with facial paralysis. The accumulation of stress and not acknowledging the good things around me left my body no choice but to force me to change. The impact of being in a constantly negative environment and around negative people only causes us harm.

We must be aware that our well-being, in whatever circumstances, should be highly considered.

I named my story "Before During After" because it expresses how I feel about my life story and how Bell's palsy changed me for the best, even if this seems impossible. My "Before" story kept my body charged with negative energy over the years, unaware of the circumstances that would happen later. My "During" story is about how Bell's palsy forced me to discover the new me and gave time back to me because now I know life is about embracing the experience of living. Being diagnosed with Bell's palsy was not easy and something I wish no one to experience. It was overwhelming as it didn't simply change how I looked, which I still have not entirely accepted, but it also changed a part of who I am. However, in my AFTER story, despite Bell's palsy changing my physical looks, my emotional side improved in the best ways possible. I was forced to learn how to make decisions that would improve my mental and emotional state, bringing healing.

One of the most notable changes in my personality is that I became more optimistic, calm, and open. I also gained a circle of friends that I love so much for their continuous support. I feel blessed for the experience of this condition. If it hadn't happened, I am sure my life rhythm from before would have caused me greater harm. The blessing of Bell's palsy coming to me at an early age taught me that life is not about academics or a career; instead, it is about living life with its fullest emotions and plans.

Life lessons come to us in many different forms. Experiencing facial paralysis from Bell's palsy was a life lesson; it taught me that life is full of emotion and wisdom, and what we do with it matters. I'm proud of my "Before During After" story, which made me a better person. I'm catching up with life and its lessons, which are plenty, and nothing is worth stressing over. We must take care of ourselves no matter the situation we encounter. Finally, I know I am a beautiful, shiny, funny girl, and I worked hard to rebuild my character, personality, and, most importantly, my life after living with Bell's palsy. In time, I hope to be back with my symmetrical face, so I can smile at the camera from all angles!

ABOUT THE AUTHOR

Maryam El Amiri is proud to come from Morocco, the land of cultures and heritage. She graduated with a Bachelor of Engineering at Al Akhawayn University. She believes that obstacles are opportunities and that it's up to her to take advantage of them and help her impact the lives of others in a positive way.

In January 2021, her facial paralysis occurred due to Bell's palsy while in her fourth year of university. The opportunity to share how she survived the recovery process with the help of her family and friends is like writing in her journal. For months, she could not express herself through the pain and could only speak one word at a time. This part of the recovery seemed endless and led to a feeling of hopelessness. She chose to write her story so others find comfort and hold onto hope during their recovery.

She loves to nap, have a lot of coffee, and spend time with her family. Also, she meditates, practices Yoga, and continues to hunt for her smile.

You can connect with Maryam at maryam.elamiri.50@gmail.com.

Connect with Maryam:

 @justmemiriam

 @maryam El Amiri

19

Silent Struggle

Kayla Tano

Big Island, HI, USA

A t thirty-three years old, my smile was wiped from my face. Never could I have imagined waking up one day and no longer having the ability to smile or blink my left eye. The once familiar face staring back at me in the mirror was now that of a stranger. Nothing could have prepared me for this, nothing. Getting the diagnosis of Ramsay Hunt syndrome (RHS) was devastating; it was as if someone had punched me in the gut, knocking my last breath out of me. I had done some research, knew what RHS was, and knew that the outcome and prognosis were poor for most, but never in a million years did I think this would be *my* diagnosis.

I've always taken pride in my physical appearance, mostly my smile. Having braces as a teen and again as an adult, my smile was very important to me. It was how I communicated with people, laughed, and expressed myself. I always took photos with a full smile showing my teeth. I took a picture with my three-year-old son about three months into recovery. At this time, my face was obviously paralyzed, with no movement and a droopy left side of my mouth. After taking the photo, my son looked at it, and then looked at me and said, "No, mama, smile like this," while taking his two little fingers, placing them in his mouth, and stretching his mouth out as wide as he could. At that moment, I knew my three-year-old could recognize something was different with my smile. It was also a painful realization that I may never get to smile in a photo with my son again; the smile I loved so much was gone.

Having facial paralysis and dealing with everyday physical challenges was a silent struggle. I felt every facial spasm and flutter, the painful dry eye, and the ear ringing while no one around me had any clue what I was going through. For me, RHS has been an isolating experience. I spent a lot of time feeling embarrassed and ashamed of my appearance, which kept me inside my house for the first four months after my diagnosis. My RHS started during a world pandemic when people were covering their faces with masks. So my dentist and physical therapist attempted to make me feel better by suggesting I wear a mask (with the idea that this would help me cope). Instead, it furthered my pain and embarrassment and was another reason to continue my isolation.

The moment Justin Bieber announced he had RHS was powerful for me. I finally had someone to relate to, and I could break free from the embarrassment and isolation RHS had caused me. I began putting one foot in front of the other and moving forward with a tiny glimmer of hope. I felt empowered when I posted a picture on social media of myself, showing my space in the internet world what I looked like, and what I had been going through. Publicly sharing was something I had not pictured myself doing before Justin Bieber's announcement. It gave me courage when he posted the video of himself with RHS.

Much attention is paid to the physical struggle of having RHS, but there is little discussion of one's mental health. At the time of writing this, I am seven months into recovery. I find myself circling around and through the five stages of grief, but I haven't landed on acceptance yet. I compare the constant change of emotions to flushing a toilet bowl and watching it go around and around, unsure which stage of grief it will land on for the day.

Some days I'm hopeful I'll get my old smile back and take that smiley photo with my son again. On other days, I'm mentally stuck swirling the bowl, feeling defeated with little hope. Then there are days in my recovery when I feel ready to step into my authentic self and move past the lingering grief. Those days, I feel motivated to use this experience to help others advocate for themselves and let them know they are not alone. But then, I'll have days when all I can do is cry and can't see past the devastation of what has happened to me. It is on these days that I have to choose to spend time grieving the loss of my face and learning to deal with the challenges it has brought me.

My facial paralysis presents different challenges every single day. Six weeks into my diagnosis, I had a gold weight placed in my left eye to help it close. Later, the gold weight was replaced with a smaller-sized platinum chain, with the goal to eventually take the weight out when my eye could close on its own. Another challenge I suffer from is synkinesis in many different forms. Synkinesis is unwanted facial movements due to incorrect nerve regrowth and is disruptive for many. My left eye closes when I chew or swallow food. It also constantly flutters while I'm awake, which, I can assure you, drives a person crazy. For context, the eye flutter is a constant spasm that can best be described as my eye dancing, except I didn't sign up to dance, and it never stops. Yet another challenge occurs when I raise my eyebrows, and the left side of my mouth is forced to pull left. For me, botox has been a blessing. It has helped with some of the synkinesis symptoms as it gives the perception of a symmetrical face, especially when at rest.

RHS has taught me to slow down and put my health first. I spent almost a week in the hospital when I was diagnosed with RHS and Mastoiditis. That week was the first time in a long time I allowed myself to stop and think about how important self-care is. I quickly realized that I had been putting myself last and not caring for myself physically or mentally for a very long time. I also discovered how much the previous few years had affected me. I am an RN who worked through the COVID pandemic and experienced severe stress and anxiety daily. Dealing with the unknowns of COVID and exposing myself, and potentially my family, to COVID caused immense anxiety every day that I went to work. My husband also lost his business during the pandemic, leaving me with the financial responsibility for our family. My stress was at an all-time high, and I believe it was the main contributor to my RHS.

The stress continued as I began to walk through recovery. The day would come when I must return to work, and this life-changing diagnosis filled me with worry, anxiety, and sadness. I didn't want to be seen; I just wanted to hide until my old face reappeared. As the time neared, worry about how my co-workers would perceive me was my constant companion, and I wondered whether I would be devalued because of my paralysis. Would people trust me to care for them with an eye that didn't blink and a lopsided mouth?

To combat some of the stress since being diagnosed with RHS, I had to decide to put myself first so that I could be there for my family *and* return to work. Until this point, my coping skills included crying and grieving the loss of my face, but then I would feel guilt over the grief. My job was to care for truly sick people. How could I be so sad over my paralyzed face when others were going through so much worse? I was in a constant emotional battle. And then, I discovered a new love, acupuncture, and began attending sessions regularly. It helped me both physically and emotionally. Thankfully, acupuncture grounded me and helped pull me out of my darkest days. I could not recommend acupuncture enough for anyone going through any facial paralysis. Exercise has been another excellent outlet for my stress and anxiety.

The most significant component in helping me cope with everything I have been through is doing things for myself and practicing self-care. I know these things will continue to help me on my journey to recover my smile. My goal is to be healthy mentally and physically so I can take care of my son and be the best mother and version of myself possible. I hope I will learn to accept my diagnosis and move forward feeling more empowered than ever. But for now, I'm learning to be kind to myself and give myself a little grace.

ABOUT THE AUTHOR

Kayla Tano has been working as a nurse for the past six years. She got her Associate degree in nursing from Hilo Community College in 2017 and her BSN from the University of Hawaii at Hilo in 2020.

In 2022, Kayla got shingles on her facial nerve causing facial paralysis known as Ramsay Hunt syndrome. She was feeling alone when she was presented with the opportunity to write for this book. Kayla wanted to connect with others who have experienced facial paralysis and share her story, and she hopes her story helps others feel supported and less alone.

Kayla is from Northern California but has lived in Hawaii since 2009. She enjoys quality time with her family, and you can often find her at the pool, beach, or browsing Target. She is a lover of all animals, especially cats.

Connect with Kayla at kaylatano@yahoo.com.

Connect with Kayla:

  kaylatano@yahoo.com

20

My Paralysis Analysis

Loriene Ezell

Seal Beach, CA, USA

M y husband yelled to me from downstairs, "How are you doing that?" I didn't know what he meant. He replied, "The crooked faces?" I had just sent him some selfies on my new phone. Concerned, he came upstairs and asked me to do several things with my facial expressions and hand movements. I thought he was nuts but did as he asked. I didn't check the mirror to see what he was concerned about or think anything was wrong because I felt okay. I told him I would lie down and rest. He agreed and left. A while later, he returned to check on me and noticed my condition hadn't changed. At this point, I had no idea what to do or where to go. I had not been to a doctor or a hospital in over fourteen years. I called and spoke to a healthcare advisor through my insurance, and after several tests at home, she advised me to go to urgent care. After five and a half long hours of waiting, I was diagnosed with Bell's palsy.

The advice given to me by the doctor was to get rest and take it easy. Instead, my life was turned upside down. My father-in-law unexpectedly passed away three days later. This tragedy left a massive hole in our family's lives. Only a few months before the paralysis, my grandchildren, who were the saving grace of life during the Covid lockdown, moved to Texas. My heart was broken, and I felt like a mess of a person. On top of losing my smile, these two significant losses almost felt like too much. It was very difficult to drive on the freeway every time I passed the exit to my grandkids' old house. I knew it would never be the same: no more pop-in visits, no more birthday celebrations, and no more holiday get-togethers. I wanted to cry but managed not to. My heart hurt, and I was numb. It had only been a few weeks, and I was still dealing with the shock that they were gone.

Unfortunately, life doesn't slow down or pause when in a crisis. I spent the following weeks trying not to let myself completely fall apart. Funeral arrangements, prepping our home for the kids to have a place to stay, and fitting our business operation into this emotionally busy time were overwhelming. Finding any quiet time for myself would not be happening soon. At that point, I really needed some comfort and peace! Not only was I dealing with a roller coaster of emotions from the loss of family and connection, but I was also struggling with the effects of Bell's palsy on my body. It caused blurry vision, dizziness, and irritation in my eyes. I found myself needing to get extra help with everyday activities like driving. It was difficult to talk as well as eat and drink. I was discouraged and distraught, but I managed to maintain my composure. I didn't want to be a burden to my family during this time of grieving, but I have to admit it was very challenging.

Being a person of faith, I found poignant Bible verses that encouraged me to keep going. Here are a few of my favorites:

- "Consider it pure joy, my brothers & sisters, whenever you "face" trials of many kinds, because you know that the testing of your faith produces perseverance." James 1:2-3

- "I am He who will sustain you. I have made you and I will carry you; I will sustain you and I will rescue you." Isaiah 46:4

- "He gives power to the faint and to him who has no might, He increases strength." Isaiah 40:29

Staying in the Word and reading Bible verses helped me to learn many things during this time. My faith was stirred up and played a vital role in helping me deal with all that came with having Bell's palsy. I was able to have a heart of gratitude for the little things like riding bikes with my husband, watching movies with the grandkids, and having spontaneous dates with friends. I learned I didn't need to "have it all together" all the time. As my family and friends lifted me up in their prayers daily, I discovered what a fantastic support team I had. Like the Bible verses, they ministered to my heart.

There have been many things in my experience that correlate to my walk with God. One of the symptoms I experienced was an increased sensitivity to sound, particularly loud voices.

- "Be still and know that I am God!" Psalm 46:10

This verse became relevant to me. I was forced to be still and hear what God was saying to me. There was nothing I could do to change my circumstances. I wasn't going anywhere. He had my full attention.

Anyone that knows me is aware that I am always on the go. Just a few years before this all happened, I was working four jobs and really stretching myself thin. I took on huge responsibilities in my church, which I thoroughly enjoyed, and grew through them all. Looking back on it through my place of stillness, I realized that maybe I could have done things a little differently.

After a few weeks, I started feeling my face around my lip moving unexpectedly throughout the morning. My jaw and the side of my face began to feel sore, and my head started to hurt. I took these symptoms as a sign of progress. On the fourteenth day, I still believed I would receive complete healing.

To take the focus off myself, I focused my attention on helping others. I found myself talking with strangers and offering them encouragement. This wouldn't have been unusual for me, except I was doing it during Covid when the whole world was scared, and human interaction was minimal.

Many people were kind and helpful toward me, and I had to learn to accept their love and help. I was used to being the person that helped others, and here I was on the other end of that stick. The whole situation was humbling, and it was hard at first to let others help me for a change. Having to wear a mask helped a lot, as I didn't want any attention drawn to my face. The first time I saw my grandkids, who had moved to Texas, I could tell they were a little alarmed by my appearance. But kids love unconditionally, and they never wavered in their love, so after I explained why my face looked fallen, they quickly went about as if nothing was wrong.

Since the Urgent Care doctor didn't give me much information, I took to the internet to get some answers and helpful advice. After about five weeks, I slowly got back into my usual routine. I returned to my spin class and work. I was able to attend six acupuncture sessions and took herbal supplements faithfully. I noticed almost complete healing by the fourth month. Yet to this day, I can feel a little weariness on the side affected by the Bell's palsy, and my eyes took the brunt of the effects.

My experience with having Bell's palsy has left me with growth and gratitude in many areas of my life, mainly spiritually and physically. Spiritually, I became more connected to God by spending more time reading His word and praying. My physical body is stronger today than in the past because I learned to stay committed to my health and not give up. I am thankful my joy was not stolen from me through this experience because I know it could have easily happened. I am surprised at how well I handled the emotions and frustrations that came with this experience. I learned to be patient and dependent on those who cared for me. I was always trying to fix things in the past and make things right on my own, but I learned that sometimes it's better to leave things alone. I am truly thankful and continue to reflect on all the good that took place during this season.

ABOUT THE AUTHOR

Loriene Ezell is a wife, mother, and grandmother and is married to Tyson Ezell. Since 1987, they have operated Ezell Company, a church, school, and office furniture distributor. Loriene has earned the title of "Life Encourager" over the last thirty-five years as she worked her way from volunteer to assistant to business administrator/wedding coordinator at her local church.

In April 2021, her facial paralysis from Bell's palsy was triggered by a weak immune system and stress. She chose to share her story to encourage others living with facial paralysis to remain strong and not lose their peace or joy. She knows her faith and confidence in God will help her to encourage those she crosses paths with in her community and life.

Loriene will celebrate thirty-five years of marriage in July 2023 and is blessed with a big family, including three granddaughters and one grandson. As a family, they share fond memories of adventures at the river. She has a passion for indoor cycling and helping others.

Connect with Loriene at lorienemezell@gmail.com.

Connect with Loriene:

   Life with Loriene

21

A Mirror and the Lens

Elena Oleske

Orlando, FL, USA

H eadshot day was here, and it was time to get ready. As a corporate recruiter who sees her fair share of professional profiles, I had set up this photoshoot for myself and my husband, Christopher. Making a first impression on others carries significant weight, and the complexities of making social connections with my fellow humans now brought an army of additional anxieties – although not all new.

Getting ready had its own challenges and rewards. I glanced at the two suits I'd chosen for the photo shoot: one blue and one pale green. The royal blue gem pressed ever so neatly on the hanger was the one I'd decided to wear first, and I couldn't put it on until I got my face in order. But suits were the easy part.

Facial issues brought on new-founded fears and insecurities. Although I'd worn makeup my whole life, it was precarious to use now since a lot could quickly go awry while applying it and washing it off. I glanced at myself in the mirror, then into my drawer of makeup (that had dwindled over time), and back up at myself, and I had to give myself a pep talk as my heart began to pound. I put the foundation applicator to my face and prayed I wouldn't inch a little too close to my eye because if I did, I would inflict pain in my cornea like Dante's inferno. Any dust from eyeshadow would do the same, so I'd become quite the contortionist while applying. Using the tip of the pad of my left index finger, I pulled down my right eyelid and pressed ever so softly on my eyelash line to hold my eye closed. Because today was photo day, a little concealer on my eyelid would help me keep that platinum weight a secret from the world. I was relieved when the final test of my artistic mastery was realized as I let go of my eyelid, and I could still see and not feel like the Mohave Desert had taken residence in my eye for the day. I skipped away and dressed in that blue suit, pretending it was my first-place ribbon.

After shifting my mental obsessions from my make-up to my outfit to my hair, I started practicing my facial expressions. Of course, this was quite a consequential day because it was photoshoot day, and I wanted to look perfect – all while having an asymmetrical face. It was quite the impossible task I had ahead of me, and as usual, I set the bar quite high. Chris needed the master bathroom to get ready, so I went to the other bathroom and mirror. As I looked at myself, I thought, practiced, and obsessed.

To say more than one person in my lifetime has accused me of being a perfectionist is quite an understatement. That trait has permeated my life, starting as a kid with gymnastics and piano. As I grew, I obsessed over musical talents and brought that same intensity to academic success in college, but I've also accomplished great things because of it.

Sure, some of my idiosyncrasies could be due to upbringing, and some perhaps genetic, but I am well aware that certain events in life also shape us.

For the past three years, I had been hiding away from the world, but It wasn't only the present-day me; there were versions of me from long ago that had also been hiding. The elementary schooler in me, who had been teased mercilessly and viciously due to pimples, was hiding – and so was the version of me from two years ago who went to see an ENT, only to be traumatized. When I stated I was having tongue paralysis issues, I was verbally attacked by a medical assistant who questioned my difficulty speaking. She scoffed at me and told me *she* had recovered quickly from Bell's palsy and had worked while having it.

Working remotely gave me that opportunity to hide from the world, yet that time also afforded me some pleasant surprises. That go-getter in me, hiding away, was still a force to be reckoned with; however, my perfectionism was mentally playing a game of tug-of-war with me. It pushed me to work hard to recover but also stifled me. Putting myself back out there to my fellow humans was essential. Setting realistic goals is good, but the unattainable goals I had set parameters for entailed returning to my former body. While yearning for it, I made these false beliefs real in my imagination. That mindset, coupled with childhood feelings of facial self-consciousness that resurfaced, was the unfortunate pairing of emotions that kept me hidden away for so long.

As I stood in front of the mirror, I practiced some of what I had learned in facial retraining. Within my first year of having facial paralysis, the obsessive person in me wanted to find the best treatment facility for synkinesis in all of Chicagoland, and I felt I did. I couldn't help but want to keep rehearsing what I had learned, and what's a little more practice going to hurt this late in the game? With every smile, I saw my eye contract. With every movement of my face from the involuntary tightening of my neck muscles to my uneven raised brow line and all the places in between, I saw only synkinesis. More self-scrutiny followed. Visions of past facial nerve retraining sessions played through my mind like a movie reel. I stared. I thought. I obsessed. Okay, relax that muscle there.

The words "the camera never lies" hold a lot of truth. Great. I was not sure I could pull this off. Good memories from the past shape us too, which was why I was thrilled to have an "ah-ha" moment. One of my most cherished mentors, Professor Garcia, from two decades past, came to rescue me from my neurotic tendencies. He had bestowed the piano wisdom that practicing before a performance would build oneself into an "anxious-obsessed state," which is why he forbade his students from practicing on recital day. That was some of the best advice I had ever been given, as it easily applied to so many of life's scenarios, and I often shared it with others.

Realizing at that moment how the payoffs of practicing a musical instrument could be likened to the gains of physical therapy/facial nerve retraining gave me a momentary boost of confidence. Both involved many painstaking repetitions of an exercise, skill, and technical ability accompanied by unwavering commitment, frustration, and moments of despair. However, this was followed by a huge reward and payoff. Sure, there were plenty of times while sitting at the piano when I didn't always like practicing scales or technical exercises, but I loved the end result of being able to play a Beethoven Sonata or Bach Prelude. Learning a new piece was always an accomplishment, and achieving benchmarks in my progress with facial retraining was the same. Knowing how I had incorporated that same work-ethic and discipline into my physical therapy, and Lord knows I had worked hard, maybe I could smile for the camera from the inside out! And with that, it was time for us to head out the door.

We arrived at the photo shoot location and met with the photographer. Immediately, he and I struck up a conversation about pianos, as he was also a certified piano tuner. We scheduled a tuning for my piano, and I felt at ease with him personally yet nervous that I was about to be photographed by a professional.

He led us into a huge modern-themed church. Some of the walls were painted cheery colors, such as orange and lime. The staircase was open and grand, and the floors were laminate and faux stone. Everyone was welcoming us, and we began to ascend the stairs. The photographer showed us where he preferred to do his headshots and explained that he would blur the background. So far, they had always come out great for photography clients. He pointed Chris and me towards the restrooms so we could fix our hair, etc. Side-by-side, we walked down the hallway looking like two board members. I still hadn't decided whether to tell the photographer about my face. I began to obsess again. Chris assured me I would make the best decision for myself. So I thought, panicked again, and then made up my mind.

Before shooting commenced, I had to come clean to the photographer; my confession had to be spoken then and there. These would be still frames of my face – frozen in time – for all the world to see. And I had been hiding away from humanity – for three years. As I stood there with all my might, as if I were about to walk in for an interview, I mustered my courage.

"So, the right side of my face is partially paralyzed. I had a severe case of Bell's palsy that never healed correctly, and I now have something called synkinesis. The nerves have re-wired on that side of my face. If we could focus on the left side of my face, that would be great!"

"What?" The photographer replied. "You had Bell's palsy? I've photographed quite a few people with Bell's palsy over the years, and I don't see anything. I almost always notice that right away. That's incredible because I look at you and don't see it."

As I stood there with my makeup, hair, suit, heels, and jewelry all prepped for this day, I felt glamorous, even if only temporarily. My glow was uncontainable and almost as bright as the colored wall behind me. I confidently stood in front of that lens and felt so much better than when I had been obsessing alone in front of the mirror.

No more hiding behind a computer screen. Enough is enough. My confidence does not rest on my physical appearance: it relies on my accomplishments and connection with others. Perseverance pays off, and I have worked hard to get where I am today through my meticulousness in finding top-of-the-line experts and spending countless hours at home doing facial retraining exercises. Never underestimate the potential you have within yourself to accomplish great things, and never underestimate the power of connecting with others. Years ago, on this journey, I became especially acquainted with Ilan and Cristina, fellow authors in this book collaborative, who have been wonderful people to know and who have been guides and friends along the way.

After this photography session, I stepped out with much more confidence and learned a few important lessons along the way. I chose to no longer wallow in the fear and self-doubt that kept me isolated for so long. Friends and family really only care about how you treat them, anyway. Sometimes, accepting a new health situation is scary, and it's more than okay to mourn for a bit, just not forever. In the years following, I was diagnosed with a rare autoimmune disease, a rare connective tissue disorder, and several other conditions. Due to my journey with synkinesis, I feel I was better equipped than I would have been otherwise in dealing with such challenges. We are much stronger, wiser, and more powerful than we give ourselves credit for, and we can learn, work hard, overcome, and succeed in life. Sometimes, we just need to take a look in the mirror and believe in ourselves.

ABOUT THE AUTHOR

Elena Oleske volunteers with various community groups and is passionate about disability education. She received her B.A. in English and Elementary Education from William Paterson University of New Jersey, graduating cum laude, and then received a second B.A. in Music. She has worked as a professional music educator in a public school setting and as a human resources professional.

Her facial paralysis occurred in December 2016, likely viral. While initially hesitant to write her story, she knew it would be cathartic for herself and a source of hope for readers, so she contributed enthusiastically. She hopes to encourage those with long-term facial paralysis or synkinesis to stay positive and never stop working on their healing journey.

Elena grew up at the Jersey Shore, met her husband in high school, lived outside Chicago for six years, and resides in Florida. She believes Chicagoland has the greatest food anywhere and also thinks shelter pets are the best. She has an affinity for music, particularly classical and classic rock, and plays piano, saxophone, sings, and composes.

Connect with Elena at contact@invisibledisabilitiesliving.com.

Connect with Elena:

 www.invisibledisabilitiesliving.com/

22

Tribute to Nature

Hailey Dougherty

San Diego, CA USA

This is a joyful story. Sure, there was a twelve-year-old American girl who came down with facial paralysis and its vexing symptoms, had to sport an eye patch on occasion, face bullies in school who picked on her *crooked* appearance, and could no longer taste Goldfish®, her most cherished salty snack. This is a joyful story not because that girl eventually experienced near complete physical recovery – which did happen over several years – but because her spirit healed. So, this is a tribute to the one who healed that part of her, a devotion to Nature, *Mother Earth, Silla,*[1] *Pachamama.*[2]

I'm Hailey. I'm that little girl, just a few mountains and valleys wiser now. As my journey to physical healing from Bell's palsy approached its final chapters, I recall ascending my favorite white oak tree overlooking the local pond. Between its branches, I consoled myself with daydreams of the inspiring adult I'd surely become as I matured.

"Soon, yes! Soon I will rise above the trauma and unabashedly share my story with anyone who will listen. I will see only beauty and bravery radiating from any pond's reflection of me. Soon, yes, soon!"

Soon never came. Don't get me wrong; if life had transpired that way, I would probably quite like it. But it has been fourteen years since my diagnosis, and I don't see my beauty in glassy ponds. Truthfully, I don't notice myself there at all, but rather something much more profoundly enchanting. Bending over fresh water, I see the shimmering scales of bluegill, ripples from a scurrying water strider, and cotton-like cattail seeds on voyages to take root. In a pond's reflection, I see Nature, the healer.

You see, while I worked diligently at physical therapy to cure my body, I took solace in Nature as I explored the growing list of existential questions in my mind. How will I express myself without a smile or frown? Can someone outwardly so different ever blend in? Was the harassment deserved? Although I felt that *people*[3] were turning against me as a "sick" kid, I noticed Mother Earth reaching out with answers. She made me feel unjudged. She was lovingly indifferent, raining or shining down equally upon me as she would my foes, the finches, praying mantises, and sweet honeysuckles.

My mother recognized the admiration that I was gaining for the natural world, and she'd beckon me to her bedroom for "sun healing." A cozy corner in her room always seemed to be kissed by sun rays. I would sit down on the carpet, face my droopy left side into a beam and summon the sun to resurrect my smile. I felt rewarded there, photosynthesizing my worries away as the warmth soothed my strained muscles after another tense day of synkinesis.

I would search for Nature, too, when she wasn't around. Sitting on another grey mat platform at physical therapy, I watched as a burning flame was placed three inches from my chin using a ruler. This *birthday candle exercise* had one instruction – blow out the flame. But, it felt far from a celebration without the ability to control my lips. As I struggled to muster a puff, I would avoid looking at the daunting, melty neon wax. Instead, I'd find peace peering at a distant painting on the wall. To this day, I can picture that whimsical impressionist cliffside speckled by pastel wildflowers.

Thanks to Nature and the love of family, I came to embrace my unique appearance and mental resilience. I felt content as fewer people inquired about my crooked smile. Perhaps that meant it no longer looked flawed. Happy to forget about the entire experience, I pocketed away my paralysis journey to collect dust.

Then, during my junior year of high school, my Environmental Science teacher, Ms. Musgrove, taught us about climate change. I had heard of the concept before, but this was the early 2000s in the state of Virginia. At that time, climate change was a hot topic, a politically controversial one often avoided in the curriculum. That didn't stop Ms. Musgrove from brazenly sharing the science of climate change nor illuminating its cause: human activities.

A warming atmosphere, rising ocean, and biodiversity loss caused by humans bullying the Earth!? This idea shook me to the core. I felt disturbed and uneasy, like suffering a relapse of the emotions I had endured from harassment. I was overcome with deep empathy for Nature, my healer.

"How much time do we have to save Her?"

That was the question I never got to ask Ms. Musgrove. Although she was a healthy, spirited young mother, she passed suddenly one day from a heart attack. This painful, unanticipated incident felt metaphorical as if it were a warning sign signifying her response to my question.

As I said, though, this is a joyful story. I decided to make it my life's work to help heal Nature as she had healed me. I studied Earth Science at university, then pursued a career in the field of global climate action and sustainable, locally-led natural resource management. In this field, I have observed devastating scenes of climate change-induced melting ice sheets in Greenland and debris from glacial lake outburst floods in Peru. I have experienced explosive wildfires in California and contracted a viral infection from mosquitos in Tanzania (expected to proliferate due to rising temperatures). However, through my global explorations, I have also witnessed the remarkable goodness of humankind as we design and pursue solutions. And I've noticed a widespread and growing collective realization that we must live harmoniously with Nature. We are restoring forests, mangroves, and peatlands. We are expanding renewable energy technology and regenerative agriculture practices, and empowering indigenous peoples, women, and youth to design equitable, resilient, and nature-based futures for all.

You see, humans are not separate from Nature. We are a node in the web of life, tasked with reciprocally healing and loving ourselves and one another, even if we sometimes feel paralyzed.

To the children, young people, and all who are on a healing journey, whether from facial palsy or another physical or mental setback:

This little girl is encouraging you to pair visits to doctors with explorations in Nature. Splash in the rain puddles, let a sunbeam tickle your beautiful cheeks and muddy your hair with soil. Should your smile or spirit feel weakened, remember that the coastal cliffs, snow-capped mountains, singing rainforests, and sparkling seas all reflect your beauty. You are a part of the most complex web of life, one among plants, animals, fungi, and fish. You and your smile are radiating, resilient, immaculately imperfect, and deeply adored precisely as you are. Nature will show you this if you give her your attention and care. She can help to heal you, too.

---

1. Silla: Silla is the sky, wind, weather, and the primary component by which everything exists in many Inuit cultures. In 2022 in Nuuk Greenland, I learned of Silla from indigenous youth changemakers who use poetry and song to inspire global climate action.

2. Pachamama: Pachamama is a goddess, or "Earth Mother," revered by indigenous peoples of the Andes. During a trip to Peru in 2016, I learned of Pachamama from an indigenous Quechua farming community who live in the shadows of melting glaciers.

3. I recognize now that people were not bullying me and instead acknowledge that just a few mean kids were. I have thought of them often over the years, have come to forgive them, and wish upon them their own form of healing, perhaps through experiencing Nature.

ABOUT THE AUTHOR

Hailey Dougherty is a lifelong nature adventurer and an advocate for young people. She works in the climate change sector, communicating conservation work happening from Greenland's ice sheets to South Africa's wildlife preserves. Hailey has spoken at international forums and published blogs on biodiversity, climate optimism, and social justice in the green transition. She holds a BA in environmental studies from the University of Pennsylvania and certifications in social inclusion and regenerative agriculture.

At age twelve, Hailey was diagnosed with left-side Bell's palsy following sudden paralysis during sleep. Writing her chapter allowed Hailey to connect with resilient individuals worldwide and to discuss her experience of being bullied in school to reach young people living with facial palsy and offer them an optimistic lens to approach healing.

Hailey enjoys snorkeling, gardening, and cliffside running with her partner in San Diego. She frequently visits her family for nephew cuddles, escape rooms, and east coast forest walks. She believes Nature is the ultimate healer and her guide through paralysis and the global pandemic, when she hit the road for two years with friends to explore and camp in America's parks.

Connect with Hailey on Instagram /hailsdoc.

Connect with Hailey:

 /in/hdougherty6/

23

Losing Face, Gaining Grace

Cheryl Klufio (CNKD)

Tampa Bay, FL, USA

Oh, the highways and tunnels where a smile can lead!
Across five world regions which I have called "home" and in countless cities I have visited, I have discovered that the first key to people's hearts (mine included) is a genuine smile. Smiling, that universal language of human connection and warmth, opens doors and helps us feel at home with loved ones and strangers alike.

For decades, everywhere I ventured, my signature smile—wide and gap-toothed—radiated my deep-rooted love for people and places, and quickly surrounded me with friends. Then suddenly, in the Sunshine City of America's Sunshine State, my face stopped working.

Seven months pregnant with my first child, I stood before my bathroom vanity to brush my teeth, but the left side of my mouth would not budge. I brushed on, determined, and took a sip of water to rinse: a stream dribbled down my mouth, and my left cheek remained deflated. I raised my eyebrows, yet only the right one responded. I tried to puff out my cheeks, but the left remained deflated again and again. My left eye bulged with each attempt. *Was I having a stroke?* I raised my arms, and both moved just fine. So, what was happening to my face?

I called my husband in to have a look, and we conferred with my sister and father (both healthcare professionals) until the name "Bell's palsy" emerged. Never having heard of it, I frantically scoured the internet for every morsel of information I could find about this rare disease.

As it happened, I had missed early signs a couple of days prior: a change in taste and a sudden pain in the neck. Apparently, having the trifecta of being in my third trimester of pregnancy, dealing with a stressful situation (attempting to sell our house), and catching a bad cold (due to my doubly reduced immunity) made me a prime candidate not only for Bell's palsy but also for a poor recovery from it.

My husband rushed me to the ER. We both were determined that I should get the widely recommended treatment of steroids and an antiviral before the seventy-two-hour window closed. Medical research had shown this to boost the chances of a full and swift recovery from Bell's palsy.

An MRI ruled out a brain tumor, which was a relief. With the help of a book and a sharp nudge (by phone) from my obstetrician, the young doctor diagnosed Bell's palsy—"severe and complete"—and prescribed the steroids and antiviral that I had requested. One nurse assured me that Bell's palsy quickly and spontaneously resolves. "It goes away on its own in a couple of weeks," he chimed.

With those words on my mind and a prescription in my hand, I was discharged into the night, both literally and figuratively: unable to properly blink, speak, drink, or eat...unable to smile.

· · · ● · ● · ● · · ·

So, what should you do when you can no longer comfortably or effectively do any of the above? What happens when you are gawked at with alternating compassion and confusion as though you were an oddity? How do you reconcile your and your loved ones' desperate hopes for your complete and speedy recovery with the flippant dismissals of that very possibility by certain neurosurgeons and other specialists who ask why you are even there?

Well, you breathe. Everyone offers this advice, and it may seem like the most weightless, ineffectual, off-the-cuff advice possible, but you really do need to take a break and breathe. What you are going through is more challenging than anyone knows: you now have to navigate daily life and the world with a different face—a face that even *you* are not yet used to.

Show yourself kindness; show yourself grace. With compassion, give yourself permission to breathe, feel, and even grieve. Acknowledge whatever you are mentally and emotionally experiencing. Self-empathy and self-compassion are helpful companions on this journey.

You can *journey in* and master your internal world, so that you are resilient no matter what happens externally. *To face the world, you first have to face yourself.* Facing yourself is the first step when you suddenly have a different face.

And, whichever form of physical treatment you choose—whether facial retraining/physical therapy, surgery, or alternative medicine—stay optimistic about your healing. You will likely find that this positive outlook helps heal you both emotionally and physically. Abundant scientific research on positive psychology and the placebo effect has proven this, and I have personally found it to be true.

Begin building that bridge back to yourself—perhaps to an even better you than you were before—and you will be amazed at where your new smile can lead!

In that spirit, I leave you with a prose poem I earlier wrote to aid us on this journey:

I.

The truth about Bell's palsy and other forms of facial palsy is that they affect everyone a little differently. Yes, there are commonalities in some of the symptoms we see and some of the waves of emotion we ride, and yes, we do find community in standing side by side. But, at the end of the day, it is ourselves we must face.

II.

I have said that to face the world, we must first face ourselves because, in a sense, each of us *is* "the world." I have said that to truly, enduringly love others, we must first truly, enduringly *love ourselves*—that we mustn't dismiss the part of those sacred instructions we so often miss: "Love your neighbor *as yourself*." "Do unto others as you would have them do *unto you*." No, we don't get to choose to follow only half of the Golden Rule. YOU are the reference point—it all begins with YOU.

III.

So, again, I extend an invitation to you to love yourself first, in this "school" of facial paralysis that life has given us in which to rehearse. Yes, do all you need to do physically and practically, but also do the internal work that is the master key.

IV.

When we teach others about facing the world with a different face, let us also reflect on and share how we gain grace from "losing face." The thing is, every human being at one point or another in this life "loses face." *Our* saving grace is that we see it happen—feel it even—and so confront what others don't.

V.

When you suddenly can't blink or eat or drink or speak; when you are suddenly stripped of your smile and so much that you have lived on and from all this while, you are forced to sit, and breathe, and feel, and think. You come to the point where you can no longer sink. Where you learn to make that space, to find that place of Peace and Power that knows...YOUR face.

VI.

As for me,

I am learning from a sea

that shows one face

after the other—

and is still the sea;

and from a sky that looks

one way and suddenly another

—and remains the sky;

That I...

That I AM...

always and ever...expanding

into the ALLness

of me.

Join me.

Whatever your path, dear friend, I wish you grace.

ABOUT THE AUTHOR

Cheryl Klufio (CNKD) created the pioneering program, "Gain Grace: Connect & Communicate with Confidence after Bell's Palsy/Facial Paralysis," to help herself and others better navigate the social challenges of facial palsy.

Cheryl is a communications leader who has served at Harvard University, Microsoft Corporation, and Chesamel Communications, among others. She is the founder and president of RightlySaid, which specializes in perfecting communication. Her credentials include a BA in literature from Mount Holyoke College (United States), an MBA and a Blue Ocean Strategy certificate from INSEAD (France and Singapore), and TEFL certification from IATQUO (United Kingdom).

Cheryl suffered a severe and prolonged case of Bell's palsy beginning during pregnancy. Having found comfort in others' stories at the time, she contributed a chapter to this book collaboration to share her journey to a better self and hopefully help others on theirs.

A Ghanaian-born global citizen who loves to travel, learn, and share as she connects with people worldwide, Cheryl is also a poet and photographer. She delights in her amazing daughter, Adora, and her wonderful husband, Nkosi.

Connect with Cheryl:

○ /beyondbellspalsy

⊕ http://gaingrace.com/

⊕ www.cherylklufio.com

THE HUNT *for my* SMILE

Resource Page

The authors of *The Hunt for My Smile* created a list of resources to help those new to facial paralysis know that there are resources out there to help in your recovery process.

They have made recommendations for:

- Medical Professionals
- Treatments and Services
- Products and Supplies

We have made this a special FREE resource located online so that it can always stay up to date.

Scan below to check out the list and print a PDF.

www.amysameck.com/HFMSResourcePage

FOUNDATION FOR
FACIAL RECOVERY

AMY SAMECK
PUBLISHING

Bell's Palsy Talk
with *Barb*
xo

Special Thanks to the

FOUNDATION FOR FACIAL RECOVERY

Your support was essential to get this book published.
Thank you.

Educates healthcare providers, patients, and the public about effective treatments for facial palsy and TMD disorders.

Their Vision: We are working toward the day when every person afflicted with facial palsy or TMJ disorders can receive expert care from healthcare professionals who understand the complexities of these conditions, are willing to take action early and often, and have an educated, current approach to pursuing full recovery.

Jodi Barth, PT, and Gincy Stezar, PTA, were honored with the 2018 Outstanding Physical Therapist/ Physical Therapy Assistant Team Award by the Board of Directors of the American Physical Therapy Association (APTA). This award recognizes Jodi and Gincy's exceptional contributions to the association and its components.

Check out the Foundations Book:

Fix My Face

Expert Advice for Maximizing Recovery from Bell's palsy, Ramsay Hunt syndrome, and other Causes of Facial Nerve Paralysis.

Found on Amazon or the Foundations website:

www.foundationforfacialrecovery.org/

ACKNOWLEDGMENTS

When Ramsay Hunt struck, I never thought I would be grateful to have met it, but here I am three and a half years later, about to give thanks for this beast of a virus. I've written for one book and published another- both facial paralysis related and pushing me to do big things with my life. Without you, RHS, the idea for this book would not have happened. So for that, I am grateful to wear the lasting effects you left on my face and life. I do hope never to meet you again, though.

Jodi Barth and The Foundation for Facial Recovery. I'm proud as a peacock to have accomplished what I set out to do, and your offer to support publishing this book leaves me eternally grateful that you had faith in my idea. Thank you for making this happen.

Barbie Wharton. You responded to my out-of-the-blue IG message when you could have just ignored it. Your strong belief in using your voice to impact the world allowed you to see my vision clearly. We clicked in our first chat, and I value the friendship and partnership that developed throughout this process. Beyond that, you are like magic with graphic design and passionate about making a difference!

Erika Harston Noll. Your editing skills made this book and the words of my first-time authors ready for the world to read. I'm not sure you (or any of us) knew what we were in for when we said "YES" to this project, but you rocked it! You carefully read our words and spiffed them up, so our ideas weren't lost in errors. Your work is the unsung hero, and I'm exponentially grateful for your time and expertise.

To each and every one of the twenty-three authors, I send the biggest, most grateful thanks from the bottom of my heart for eagerly jumping on board this project. You accepted the invitation to write a chapter about your experiences, even though I was a stranger, albeit a sister in tragedy who understood much of what you had been through. You shared my desire to fill the literary gap and wanted to be a part of creating a resource that would help not only those living with facial paralysis but also their friends and loved ones. You trusted me, full stop.

To my personal supporters. There's no good way to put these names down in order of importance because each one made a difference and impacted my process to get to the point where this book happened.

My family: Ma/Carol, your gentle spirit and big heart never stopped encouraging me. Jacob and family, I felt your love and support. Dad/Jack, your encouragement to never quit and always trust in God helped on days when it felt hard. You might not have understood where I was going, but you always supported and trusted I would find my way. And this isn't just in relation to the book.

My Sister and Friend, Abby. Your unwavering support and consistent reminders that I could do this kept me going more than a few times, especially at the end, when fear and doubt kept wanting to creep in (you pulled me back from the brink a few times). I am grateful for your help, trust, and belief in me. You're also an incredible business coach!

My 15+ year friends: Brooke, Sharon, Dina, and lifelong friend, Sonia. Y'all have been there through the highs and lows. When life got thrown off track and I needed time to figure out my next steps you were there and never let me walk the journey alone. Socks/Loved You.

My Ella. No other words describe you. Those closest to me know who you are in my life, and this book would never have happened without you! WEIP?

I saved the best for last. To my two most precious believers- Taylor and Jonah (can't forget our puppy, Megatron, who joined us halfway through this journey). Your support, love, and belief in me mean everything. I did this as much for me as I did for you. Your kind eyes don't see the wonky smile or winky eye. They just see me, and through the haze of teenagerdom, they love me. So always remember that where there is a will, there is a way. It may take time, and it will certainly take effort, but stay humble and kind, and work hard, and you can achieve anything you put your mind to. You are my sunshine, and I Love You More / IW.

Amy S.

THE HUNT *for my* SMILE
Also By Amy

The Truth About Finding Joy in the Darkness

Want to know how it all started? This book is the precursor to *The Hunt for My Smile* and was released in the fall of 2021.

I share my story of paralysis and how I overcame the early days of pain, sorrow, and devastation. It's also a collaborative written by nineteen women who share their stories of triumph over tragedy and how they did it with JOY! Every chapter is a fantastic story of survival and success.

Go to **www.amysameck.com**
to learn more.

Coming Back Soon!

The Reminiscence Journal

Not currently in print, but this journal will be back soon and is a three-year project that asks thought-provoking questions, with a touch of humor and inspiration, and acts as a journal, diary, or memoir that can be passed down to loved ones so they can get to know you better.

www.amysameck.com

AMY SAMECK
PUBLISHING

Made in United States
Orlando, FL
23 March 2023

31353876R00124